How
Winning Non-Fiction

How To Write Winning Non-Fiction

The Complete Writing and Publishing Handbook for Non-Fiction Authors

Suzan St Maur

First Published In Great Britain 2010
by Publishing Academy
www.publishingacademy.com

To Leah

…my cousin, born 2009

*I hope you will write a book
of your own one day,
and that this book
will still be around
to help you.*

Contents

Praise

"It's all here: everything you need to write winning non-fiction...from what types of non-fiction sell, how to write it, who to talk to, what to say, and what not to say to how to get the best deal from a publisher...oh and let me throw in a sample contract, sample letters and a list of contacts to get you started...and if you need anything else, just give me a shout. What more can you ask for?

"Friendly...up to date...brilliant, if you're looking for a one-stop, simple to understand masterclass on writing winning nonfiction, getting published and earning a few bob in the process, this is it."
Martin Duffy, Martin's Miracle, www.martinsmiracle.co.uk

"This book is a must for all those people who have the urge to write an informative book. Written with humour and above all, extensive knowledge, it is the perfect guide for the first time writer. All aspects are covered to not only channel you in the correct direction but to also give you the confidence to know how to approach the publishing industry. I wish that this book had been about on the start of my journey to being a published author as it answers so many questions from the very start."
Ginny Oakley, Co-author, 'What Not To Wear On A Horse'

"I love this book. Easy to read. Easy to understand. Easy to put into practice. Once again Suzan St Maur has written a book that provides support and motivation to people who want to write non fiction and it couldn't have come at a better time. From composing a title to looking after your ideas, Suze has great tips to help you get your work of non fiction into the hands of the public. Thanks a million Suze, this has made a big difference to the way I write."
Sarah Arrow, Editor, 'Birds On The Blog',
www.birdsontheblog.co.uk

Foreword

I knew Suze well before I ever met her because of the huge body of published books she's written over the last couple of decades.

One of her books in particular, 'Writing Words That Sell', published way back in 1991 had such an impact on my own writing that when I finally did get the chance to connect with her, it felt like one of those "meet your idol" moments.

I was just fourteen in 1991 and didn't read Suze's book, let alone know what copywriting really was, until I was working as a copywriter myself six years later. But, I can tell you I owe a lot of my own writing success since to Suze and that one book.

And that's just one of the great things about writing and publishing non-fiction; your words and teachings can span time and generations to impact those who wish to follow in your footsteps.

Of course, Suze has been published many times by publishers with far more credibility and kudos than our little outfit and, with that in mind, I can think of no better mentor for would-be authors and budding non-fiction writers.

Suze, with her savvy, no-nonsense approach to writing, has inspired me and countless others and I'm sure she'll do the same for you with this book.

**Joe Gregory, co-author of 'The Wealthy Author'
and co-founder of The Publishing Academy,
www.publishingacademy.com**

Introduction

Even if you are a professional writer to start with (as I am) the thought of writing your first entire book can be terrifying. I know I was terrified when I began work on my first book.

Since that time, I got over my fear and am now hovering (at the time of writing this) just over the 20 published nonfiction titles mark. Those have been completed over a period of just over 20 years – so almost one a year on average. In addition to producing the books I have also been working on commissioned business as a corporate/marketing/consumer/healthcare writer, running a house, giving birth to and bringing up my son, caring for my elderly (now late) parents, plus a few other things. And I'm still sane enough to tell the tale without tearing my hair out.

Conclusion: writing nonfiction books does not have to be a lengthy, arduous exercise. It can fit in with the rest of your life. It can – and should – be fun.

Of course, writing does not come easily to everyone, but everyone can improve their writing skills by getting plenty of practice. You may find that before you tackle your first book, you could warm up your skills by writing articles on your topic, and/or writing a blog about it. In fact many nonfiction books – especially of the "how to" variety – have started out as a collection of articles on a topic or, indeed, have been derived from a popular blog.

What helps you more than anything else is if you enjoy writing your book. I can't teach you to enjoy it, but in the following pages I hope you'll find plenty of

1

information, tips, shortcuts and other tools that will help you write your book much more easily than were you to attempt it on your own. That should leave you free to have a great time doing it!

Suzan St Maur
www.suzanstmaur.com

CHAPTER 1

The Nonfiction Picture Today

The entire international book publishing scene has changed a lot in the 21st century. Whereas becoming a published nonfiction author was difficult even until the end of the 20th century, now it's easy due, largely, to the vastly increased number of different publishing options, not to mention an increase in delivery options – print, eBook reader, audio book, etc.

Undoubtedly, the fact that producing and publishing a book has become a) easier and b) cheaper makes the whole book market more accessible to wannabe authors. Consequently there are literally millions of books for sale out there, and not all of them are good.

However, the goalposts have been moved in recent times. Although in the past the only criterion for the publication of a nonfiction book was its literary and/or informational merit, today not all books are published with a view to becoming best sellers so they don't have to be "good" by mainstream publishers' standards. Many of these books are published (usually self-published) as marketing tools and as the means to a PR or promotional end, rather than as little profit centres in their own right, and are sold and/or distributed to audiences other than the general public.

What all this means, then, is that depending on your reasons for wanting to write a book, its concept and content don't necessarily have to conform to traditional mainstream publishing values. Don't forget, though, that whatever you want your book to achieve, it has to be good – "fit for purpose," as the saying goes. If your book is bad, it will make you look bad.

As you will see from the pages that follow, the actual writing of a book does not have to be difficult or expensive. Provided that you can talk coherently, you can write a book – with help, perhaps, but you *can* do it. And the best news is that these days the help you need, should you need it, is much more available – and affordable – than ever before.

However before we get into *how*, let's first go into the *why*.

Nonfiction Books & The Market For Them

It seems that every time you ask a publisher how the nonfiction/business book market is doing, they will say that it's awful. However when you check out actual book sales the picture looks different. Perhaps we should conclude that it's publishers who are having a hard time, not books. Many publishers still hang most of their sales opinions on what happens in bookstores too, which these days are not where most people go to buy business and other practical nonfiction books.

Business books get a particularly hard time in bookstores. In most of the bookstores I go into these titles are crammed into a few shelves on the top floor way over at the back by the entrance to the employees' toilets. Bookstore managers don't like the people who seek business books because they tend to browse a lot and buy little – hence the self-defeating policy of putting these books by the toilets. I'll never understand their merchandising policy. Even in other bricks-and-mortar retail environments like office supplies superstores – where you would think there's a good market for business books – you'll find them stashed away between the waste paper baskets and the giant cans of instant coffee.

I believe people prefer to buy business and practical nonfiction books from related retail outlets, offline catalogues, or online. This isn't the place to go into lots of statistics, but in the UK, vast quantities of nonfiction books are sold in places like supermarkets, garden centres, gift shops, newsagents/ stationers, DIY stores, office supply stores, etc., as well as the various online sources. But because publishers have huge amounts invested in the heavy overhead of distributing books to bricks-and-mortar bookshops, they hang on to that with their fingernails.

Some publishers are changing the way they do business, but I believe they still have a long way to go. Mainstream publishers are also being squeezed by the rise in the number of self-published nonfiction books on the market and increasingly these self-publishers are getting their books into the main distribution channels.

Technology, too, is making the whole book publishing industry take a rather nervous look at itself. As I write this Amazon's Kindle electronic book reading device has just become available in the UK and already there are several competitors in that emerging market. Despite the manufacturers and distributors of the devices and their associated software proclaiming that piracy of books won't be possible, needless to say we authors are becoming very twitchy about it.

Suzan St Maur

Already we have seen how the whole pattern of the music industry has changed, largely due to piracy, free downloads, etc., and now if you're a musician and want to make a living, the only way is by "gigging" – bums on seats in concerts. "Record sales," as they used to be known, have been hugely devalued. Unlike musicians – who at least have their live performances as a product to sell – many of us nonfiction authors need to hang on to book sales, because without those there is nothing else. Unless, of course, you fall into the category of writing a book as a promotional tool for your business – see below.

However, the printed book is not dead yet. Historically technology has not really revolutionized society quite as much as had been predicted. Despite all the predictions, radio did not get killed off by television. Despite many further predictions, the internet has not killed off newspaper and magazine sales. And despite (perhaps commercially biased) predictions now, I doubt that electronic book readers will replace paper-printed books. Would you really want to take your Kindle to read from when you're in the bath, on the toilet, on a beach, in bed, under a tree, in a hammock, etc.? I wouldn't. But then a) I'm a nonfiction author and b) I'm a confirmed Luddite and technophobe.

Let's not get carried away here, taking pot shots at the messenger when a more cheerful message is staring us in the face: whatever the media used to deliver them, there will always be a market for books. People have a craving for knowledge (nonfiction) and for entertainment/escapism (fiction) and nothing is going to change that. Onwards and upwards!

So Why Write A Nonfiction Book?

Well, to begin with there aren't many more effective promotional tools. "Having a book published" still holds a certain kudos and perhaps in Pavlov-dog fashion, people automatically associate someone who writes a book about something with that someone being an expert on the subject.

In the USA, one prolific speaker on business topics has been heard to describe his books – which he self-publishes – as "$30 business cards." Cynical perhaps, but the folklore about the author of a book being an expert in his/her field still works. The "$30 business card" gets you recognised as an expert even, Heaven forbid, if you don't deserve to be.

If you work as a public speaker (even part-time) or as a trainer, lecturer, motivator, instructor, actor, comedian, musician, or in fact whatever occupation that gives you access to captive audiences – a book is a useful product. After your performance, presentation, workshop, seminar or course you can sign copies of your book for members of your audience and provided the price isn't too high, you'll sell a good few copies.

Alternatively you can incorporate a "free" copy of your book for each delegate into the package for organisations booking your presentation or training course, thereby adding quite a lot of perceived value.

Particularly if you're a musician, actor or other celebrity, your biography or autobiography will sell very nicely alongside your CDs, DVDs and other merchandise.

A book also makes a good addition to your product range, if you're selling "back of room" from a lecture or seminar or after a concert, performance, or whatever, because it gives you something to "bundle" with your other merchandise and therefore make an attractive package. For example, if you're a musician with an album to sell on CD, after a live show you can sell the following options:

1. Your CD for, say, £15

2. Your book for, say, £10

3. Your new CD *and* your book ("bundled" together) for just £20!

You may not double your merchandise sales via option #3, but you definitely will increase them overall. Most people find it hard to resist a bargain. Also, the launch of your book will create publicity opportunities for you that you wouldn't otherwise get with a CD alone, so the sales activities of both products should be symbiotically beneficial.

Used correctly, your book will also be a helpful PR tool in other areas, and will make a gift that has a very high perceived value.

Depending on which publishing route you choose your markup on the direct sales of your book will vary, but even if your profit margin is relatively low, book sales will still enhance the overall marketing success of whatever you do, add to your reputation as an expert in your field, and get your messages and ideas out there where you want them to be. For more on the financial issues – and gains to be had – connected with writing and publishing nonfiction books, take a look at "The Wealthy Author" by Joe Gregory and Debbie Jenkins... details in Chapter 17.

CHAPTER 2

What Does Your Book
Need To Be Successful?

With nonfiction books the question of whether or not
to write one has to be a business decision. It needs to
be taken in the same way as a decision to introduce a
new product or service. With nearly all nonfiction (and
fiction too, up to a point) there is usually room for a
good new book on the market, provided it's likely to
attract a substantial group of readers because:

- It's about something entirely new and very
  interesting that no-one has written about
  before

...or...

- It's about something that's not new, but to
  which you contribute something entirely new
  and very interesting

If you are going to find a conventional publisher to do
your book you will need to write some very
convincing proposals about your concept, along the
lines of these two points. Even if you decide to go the
self-publishing route you still need to fulfill either of
those points. That's because when you come to
market your book, you will need to be able to
convince the distributors – and of course the
potential purchasers – that your book is worth
stocking and buying.

Whatever happens be brutally honest with yourself,
because if you aren't, a potential publisher – and

potential readers – certainly will be. If the answer is still "yes," then go ahead… and good luck!

If You're An Expert, Go For It

Even if there are several books on the market already about your particular area of expertise, don't be intimidated. The topic itself might be well known but your views and personal take on it aren't – especially if your input is surprising, unusual, controversial or breaking new ground in some way. That's good enough to make the book of interest to its readership, whatever publishing method you use.

Make Something Easier

If your book offers a process, tips, shortcuts and other ways in which readers can achieve something they need to achieve more easily/quickly/cost-effectively, it will do well. Especially (but not necessarily) if you are a known expert in your topic, you may well be surprised at how much valuable knowledge and experience you have ready to share with others less accomplished than you are. Often people don't realise how much expertise they have until they sit down and think about it. You may have created shortcuts and new methods without really noticing them. Yet to a beginner in that area, these could be worth their weight in gold, saving them a great deal of time, effort and even money.

Give Readers Pleasure

Nonfiction books with a feelgood factor will nearly always do well, because people like to feel good about themselves while they're absorbing the information you share with them. Whether you write about delicious food and wine, beautiful-but-simple embroidery and needlework, DIY car repairs, social networking, aromatherapy or whatever, you book needs to exude a positive, smiling atmosphere. Negative stuff does not normally sell. One of my weddings books, "The A to Z of Wedding Worries and how to put them right," has sold very few copies to brides and brides' families as it was intended to originally. Silly *moi* – I should have thought of that. What bride wants to face up to – and pay money for - the fact that she may encounter problems in her wedding preparations, even though it's 90 percent certain that she will? Luckily for me and the publisher the wedding planning industry is rather more hard-nosed about the whole issue and the book is selling well within that market!

So it's positive, positive, all the way.

Inspire & Change Lives

Many people are dissatisfied with their lives and are attracted to books which tell them how to revolutionise things, from their love lives to their relationships at work to cleaning and de-cluttering their homes. If you have specialised knowledge that you know transforms life for people around you, and/or if you have developed a life-changing process for yourself, unless it's about something incredibly obscure people will want to read about it. Even in our increasingly cynical age where you can rent gurus by the metre, readers always want more help to try to realise their dreams. If you believe you can help them, genuinely, then write your book.

Entertain

There is no rule that says even a serious textbook has to be written in a dull and boring way. It's a fact of life that no matter how interesting or informative the subject matter, if it is written in a turgid and lumpy style readers will find it hard going. If they scan the book in the bookstore or online before buying it, that turgid and lumpy style may well be enough to make them pick someone else's book. There's plenty more about writing style and craft in Chapter 14, but right from your book's inception, you need to think in terms of letting readers enjoy the experience of reading it. Think in terms of sharing your information with a friend over a drink or a cup of coffee. Be informal and conversational. Use humour if you want to. Make sure those thoughts set the tone for your book, right from the beginning.

CHAPTER 3

How To Get A Good Idea

If you haven't quite formulated what you want to write about or how to approach it, you'll need to get your thinking cap on and come up with some ideas.

Many people imagine that good ideas appear by magic, like those cartoon light bulbs that switch themselves on over a character's head with a caption that reads "Eureka!"

Okay, inspiration can happen spontaneously. But what most people don't realise is that there are thought processes and mind-triggers you can use to feed and nurture your imagination... ways to ensure you spot opportunities and make sure that inspiration happens. In the case of many, many businesses and non-business activities, creative inspiration comes about through method - not madness.

Nowhere does this apply more vigorously than in my own background as an advertising copywriter. In that business, you need to have good ideas on demand. Multi-million spend advertising clients do not expect to wait around until light bulbs switch on over the "creatives'" heads. Ideas, and damned good ones, are required on schedule. It's "I want a new campaign by Monday morning - or else." Happily you're unlikely to find yourself under this kind of pressure, which in some ways is a shame... it's surprising how well that pressure can work!

Opportunity Spotting

A key trigger for creative inspiration is opportunity spotting.

Think Dyson vacuum cleaners: paper bags were fiddly, dirty to handle and tended to break. Solution? Bagless vacuum cleaner.

Think no-frills airlines: all this paraphernalia of fancy meals, drinks, snacks and lavish pampering by a large group of grinning cabin crew was a hangover not only from 1950s and 1960s commercial air travel, but also from ocean liner travel even before that. It made modern air travel too expensive. Solution? Get rid of all but the essentials and make airfares more affordable.

Think sushi bars: people – especially in the USA – grew to love Japanese food, and hey presto, it just so happened that it could be made quickly and theatrically. Solution? Combine the concept of that with the popular fast-food culture.

And so-on. The people behind these good ideas followed processes to gain inspiration and use it profitably – from entrepreneurs to engineers, from scientists to artists, from writers to inventors.

There is the potential for expensive mistakes here though, so read on...

Avoid Solutions That Are Looking For Problems

The sadly pot-holed roads of many developing countries could be repaired and paved successfully with solutions to problems that don't add up to a row of beans in real life.

For an example of how that works we should look at the IT industry in the 1970s and 1980s. This was in the era when techies swanned about in white coats working in air-conditioned buildings closed to anyone without a PhD in wizardry. They were paid to come up with great ideas for magic boxes which would then be sent over to the sales and marketing wallahs with a message saying, "here's an M-9-24 Version X. It does this, this, and this. Now go and sell it."

In those days when most of us were in awe of technology, the method worked; businesses and other organisations didn't have very much at all in terms of information technology to make things run more efficiently so in a sense, anything was better than nothing. However once IT had become more common, customers became increasingly picky until one day the MD or CEO of some relatively important organisation turned around to their IT suppliers and said, "I don't care how the box works or how many widgets it has; what will it do to improve my bottom line? And I want the damned thing to speak English, not computer gibberish, so you had better change all that crap that appears on the screens so I can understand what it's achieving for us."

Shock, horror!

For the first time in history, the IT industry was obliged to become "customer-focused." No longer could the IT giants of the era come up with magic boxes that achieved what their engineers thought was a cool performance and then expect their customers to find something useful to do with them. No longer would customers buy solutions that were looking for problems. And those of you who are old enough to remember the way the IT industry went through a throat-grabbing culture change in and around the 1980s will know what – and who – I'm talking about.

Whether we writers of nonfiction books like it or not, we – like any other purveyor of a product or service offered to a market – must be "customer-focused," too. Of course, there's nothing wrong with writing an almost-certainly self-published book about your Auntie Beryl's knitting patterns or 379 different presentations of ingrown toenails, provided that you regard it as a personal achievement and don't expect it to be either a commercial success in the book market or a useful PR tool for your business. OK, unless you have an audience of knitters or podiatrists, I suppose. But you get my drift?

I think it's a cruel truth to say that no matter how good you think your idea is, you need to conduct some sort of reality check before developing it beyond a single thought. Some people worry that if they discuss their idea openly someone else might steal it and do it themselves. Sadly this is true; it happens. That's a hard fact of life and we have to get over it; more on this topic below. But 99 percent of the time your ideas will not get pinched and even if they do, whoever pinches them won't have your unique expertise and slant on the subject. A reality check conducted with people whose views you trust and respect is only a very small risk, and it's well worth taking.

Anticipate The Book's Future

Something I see quite frequently in my work as a book editor is the way new nonfiction authors often forget that a book has a long shelf life. Long chunks of a book – or even the basic idea for the book in the first place – will be based on "here and now" circumstances that will be significantly different in a short time. You may be fed up to the back teeth with your country's current president or prime minister and write about it, but someone reading this further down the line may only recall that person as ancient history. A current climate of economic gloom – or boom – will almost certainly not be present in a few years' time.

This doesn't mean to say you can't write an excellent book about a current event or issue, but simply be mindful of the fact that people are likely to be reading it anything up to several years after you write it. (Some of my books are still being borrowed from public libraries over 20 years after I wrote them.)

Issues that can date a book are any that are relatively transient in our lives and/or that are subject to fairly regular change, e.g.:

- Politicians
- Politics
- Governments
- Laws
- Economic circumstances (e.g. recession)
- Fashions
- Prices
- Technology
- Cars
- Some health issues
- Education
- Etc.

Brainstorming

Brainstorming has been around as a quick-fix way to generate ideas for a long time now, and even has been teleported into the hi-tech age with such methodology as Tony Buzan's "Mind Mapping." Both hand-written and electronically generated spider charts and various other systems have been developed which formalise what many people had been doing for decades anyway, which basically involved doodling on a piece of paper.

Verbal brainstorming is popular, too, especially in its form of "think tanks" and "retreats" often used by corporations and other organizations to whip their people up into a frenzy of new ideas that ultimately will benefit the organization, and – we assume – the recipients of its services.

Whatever method suits you, beware of brainstorming for new ideas when the ground rules have not been set properly. I remember being asked to attend a brainstorming session for a very large chain of estate agencies (real estate brokers) some years ago. They had developed various new, hi-tech methods which bypassed many of the traditional ways of buying and selling homes and as such wanted to promote their uniqueness in a video. I was brought in by the production company to attend as the writer/producer and help them develop their thoughts.

After a very early start and a long drive I arrived at their offices in one of England's loveliest northern cities, to find the group of company staff looking slightly haggard and worn after two hours' debate over the bacon rolls and coffee. I was presented with a long list of reasons why their service was better than everyone else's. Not wishing to wee-wee on their bonfire but also not wishing to spend the following two days there, I said, "OK, that's great. But what is it we're really doing here, with all these features that make the process easier?"

Blank looks all around.

"Isn't it that we're taking the stress out of buying and selling your home?"

Blank looks. Followed by smiles. And what had I done? Merely turned around that hairy old chestnut of features versus benefits. Now, because we were no longer looking at features, we could come up with ideas that were benefit-led and therefore far more likely to grab our audience.

Brainstorming is great – provided you set it up right. Remember, what we don't need is solutions looking for problems.

What Problems Need To Be Solved?

Having warned you about the dangers of solutions looking for problems, whatever you do, don't assume there aren't any problems to solve. There are plenty. What you need to do in your search for a good idea for your book, is to ensure that you keep your eyes open for real problems in your particular market or topic area, and keep aware of what's missing from whatever options there are currently to solve those problems.

Time, probably, is on your side. Solutions put forward to problems 10 or even 5 years ago, may no longer be appropriate and may indeed have been superseded by better solutions. Your solution might be even better still.

What Are You Really Good At?

This may seem obvious, but have you really thought the uniqueness of your idea through? You know all there is to know about your topic, but in all fairness there may be other experts out there who are in the same position.

What is unique about you, though, is what will sell your book. You may not even be aware that your ideas on your topic are unique, but hey – have a look back through your earlier musings, notes, essays, articles, papers, speeches, presentations, etc. I'd put money on the fact that you have an unique take on your topic. Find it, develop it, and make it happen.

Be Nosey

If you have even the inkling of an idea for a nonfiction book, don't be shy. Get out there and try your idea out. Ask around. You have a great deal to gain by sniffing around whatever sources you can to seek out to see whether your idea – or your germ of an idea – is worth taking further. Look for problems, in your area of expertise, that need solving – *really* need solving. Those can appear when you least expect it so be vigilant. And keep asking around!

Watch Your Topic

This may seem glaringly obvious, but once you have an idea for a nonfiction book you need to watch very carefully to see what is being discussed about that particular topic. Or, should your idea be moving into uncharted waters, you need to keep abreast of everything that might be relevant.

Online Resources

At the time of writing, Google Alerts are a very useful tool that can help you keep up with your topic all over the world. You simply set up however many words or phrases relevant to your topic that you want, and Google will email you whenever they are mentioned on the internet. It's a free service, too. Obviously you need to be fairly precise in what words or phrases you search for if you don't want to receive a lot of irrelevant stuff along with the good bits.

The Google Alerts set up page gives you a good choice of options, so just follow their instructions – see box. You'll find it online here: *www.google.com/alerts*

Another helpful tool is Google AdWords. This is intended to help advertisers find out which key words and phrases, relevant to their product or service, are being searched for on Google, and in which volumes. It can be useful when checking out an idea, as well, because the results will give you an indication of overall interest in that idea or topic. To find it, Google "google keyword tool."

Of course, the whole of Google and most other search engines are available to you and it's well worth monitoring your topic or idea on a weekly or monthly basis while you're developing it. Similarly, keep checking on Amazon to see if related books are being published and if so, how well they are doing on the Amazon Sales Rank.

Cuttings

Cutting articles out of newspapers and magazines may seem like a rather charmingly old fashioned thing to do these days, but it's amazing how many authors still do it whenever they read something that either triggers an idea for a book, or adds substance to an idea they are already playing around with.

In fact it's probably worth packing a small pair of scissors in your briefcase or bag when you're out and about, to make the process easier than tearing! (Avoid taking them in your hand luggage when you're flying, though, or the security people may think you want to stab the pilot...) You never know when you'll see an article that you want to keep hold of – it's just as likely to be while reading the paper on a train, or a magazine in the dentist's waiting room, as it is when you have deliberately set out to research something.

Needless to say you can get reasonable results from searching online versions of national and local newspapers, magazines, etc., then creating a "cuttings file" on your computer. However bear in mind that the contents of online and offline versions of publications are not always the same, and online versions often tend to be shorter and less detailed.

Protecting Your Idea

There is a very short and not very pleasant answer here: you can't. You can copyright titles, texts, poems, novels, etc., and you can trademark a logo or name, but until an idea is expressed and recorded in some considerable detail you can't stop somebody else developing and exploiting it, or at least something very similar to it.

Once upon a time – at around the time that food intolerances became fashionable - I came up with a nifty idea to develop a range of dairy-free and gluten-free food products. Like a good citizen I consulted my friendly local Business Link advisor who said, "great idea, forget it." When I asked why he said, "because your potential distributors, like supermarkets, will sit back and watch while you spend a fortune on developing the products, get a few samples from you, make the products themselves with small differences in names and ingredients, and then tell you to **** off."

Another time I came up with an idea for a documentary series for one of the main TV channels in the UK. I made four consecutive presentations to so-called "commissioning editors" (who turned out afterwards to have been freelance, independent producers) who liked the idea very much. Then I heard nothing. 12 months later the channel aired a series using not only my idea, but even my title... the only thing they had changed was whereas I had suggested featuring three men and three women, they had six women. Although I had what seemed like a valid case, I was advised that should I try to take legal action they would mess me around with their expensive lawyers until I ran out of money.

I know, it's a dog-eat-dog world out there.

It's often a case of striking a balance. On the one hand you want to run your idea past sufficient people whose opinions you value, and this is a very important part of your development and refinement processes. On the other hand, though, you don't want to talk about your idea in a busy pub, bar, restaurant or even bus or train, because you never know who might be listening.

And even if you write up your idea in some detail, it won't necessarily be enough to prove it's yours in a court of law. When I had my run-in with that TV channel (see above) my idea ran to a 20 page proposal with skeleton scripts of each episode and a full production and post-production budget.

Essentially, the only real protection you can get is if your idea, and your book, could only possibly be developed and written by you... and that anyone else couldn't do it successfully without you.

So... use your uniqueness!

Collating Your Ideas
Finally, never discard an idea which you like, even if – on researching it – you find there isn't a market for

it. There may not be a market for it at the time, but this can and often does change.

As I write this, I have three other book concepts in negotiations with publishers. One is 15 years old, the second is 9 years old, and the third is 4 years old. The first two are novels and neither tickled any publishers' fancies when I first came up with them, but now I have a publisher wanting to do both. Their concepts – the ideas behind them – have become fashionable.

Keep your ideas in an actual or virtual folder, in a nice safe place, and keep looking back through it. Not only can an old, undeveloped idea suddenly become flavour of the month, but also old ideas can often trigger new ones.

Suzan St Maur

CHAPTER 4

Creating A Book Title

All book titles (fiction as well as nonfiction) are a very important part of the marketing of a book. With nonfiction and particularly business books, like every other piece of marketing communication should, the book title has to offer or at least suggest a benefit to the reader.

It's the title people react to when they see a book displayed, whether that's on a shelf in a bookstore or online. When people are looking through books you only have one chance to get their attention, which is why your title needs to be powerful enough to stop them in their tracks.

Another important consideration within contemporary nonfiction book sales is creating a title that's easily found by search engines, either within an online sales site like Amazon or Barnes & Noble, or on one of the general search engines like Google. Search engine optimisation (SEO) is a science in itself, but essentially you should ensure your title contains the most obvious words someone would key into a search box when looking for a book like yours. For further advice on SEO, here's a useful resource: *www.highrankings.com* To check on the keyword element of your book title you might find this resource helpful: *www.wordtracker.com* And see Chapter 3 about using Google AdWords to find out which search terms are most popularly used for your topic.

Probably the best title of all my books was "Writing Words That Sell" which I co-authored with US writer

John Butman. I have to put my hand up and admit that this was not my first choice. I can't remember what my first choice was but the editor at Lennard Books (the original publishers) told me to go away and come up with something more hard-sell. "Writing Words That Sell" stuck in my throat a bit because in those days I think I must have had delusions of grandeur, and that was a bit too hard-sell for my taste! However later on I had to eat my words (is there a metaphor in here somewhere?) because the book sold like hot cakes (still with that metaphor...) Well, for a business book it did, anyway. Everyone loved the title because it promised something worthwhile. And even though the hard cover edition was first published way back in 1989, the book is still around today.

Titles should also be simple where possible. My first book was co-authored with gemmologist Norbert Streep and was a commonsense, down-to-earth guide to buying and wearing jewellery. Norbert and I agonised for weeks over a suitable title until one day I said to him, "Norbert, how have we been referring to this thing for the last three months?"

"The Jewellery Book," replied Norbert.

"There's our title," I said. After we'd both finished laughing, we phoned the publishers and they thought it was a great idea too. It was simple and although there was no obvious promise, its simplicity suggested that it was a simple book about jewellery, which is exactly what we wanted to convey.

So the key is, simple and powerful – and preferably with a promise.

Sub-headings are quite fashionable and they help a lot to qualify the promised benefit. I've used them for several books so far and they work nicely, e.g.:

- Powerwriting: *the hidden skills you need to transform your business writing*

- Canine Capers: *over 350 jokes to make your tail wag*

- How To Get Married In Green: *have an eco-friendly wedding without compromising on style*

- Wedding Speeches For Women: *the girls' own guide to giving a speech they'll remember*

- Planning A Winter Wedding: *and how to do it in style*

If you browse through book titles on Amazon or other online sources you'll see how the subtitles work. You'll also see how attractive some titles are, and why, which will help you choose the title for your book.

Using familiar words in a new and different way, and/or in new combinations, can be a very strong approach for a book title, as long as the new word or phrase you create strongly expresses the book's promised benefit or hook. "Powerwriting" is one such example; and another book idea I had (which I want to do one day) was "Laughterology: *the science of humour and how it works for us.*"

Suzan St Maur

CHAPTER 5

Courses, Co-Authors, Ghosts & Other Spooks

There are hundreds or probably thousands of courses on the market that go into great depth about how to write almost any kind of book, fiction and nonfiction. Most of them are good. But you may not have time to wade through a long series of tutorials, or to commit to taking an online or evening course.

In all honesty 1 believe that books and courses are very helpful if you're a first-time fiction writer, because in this type of writing you need to become skilled at many tricks and technical issues that you're unlikely to have learned anywhere else. I'm just starting in fiction (two novels completed) and I've found two or three books on the topic which have taught me how to improve my style a lot.

But writing nonfiction is not rocket science. Pretty well any literate person should be able to assemble a reasonable draft of a business book, how-to book, etc. Then, with – or even without – the help of a professional editor, that draft can be knocked into excellent shape and emerge as a nonfiction book that's not only interesting, but also a "good read."

What you have to remember is that although courses and tutorials can teach you how to write better, they can't teach you how to share your own expertise. And the whole point of your nonfiction book is to share your expertise, not amuse readers with pretty literary prose.

Another issue that bugs me about courses on writing, is that some of them have a way of taking your morale to pieces and making you feel like you couldn't write out a shopping list, never mind write a 50,000 word book. There is such a thing as over-training. And if you over-train your writing skills you might find that your "writing personality" gets lost or diluted.

Nowadays it isn't all that important to ensure that your grammar and punctuation are perfectly polished, although you need to observe the basics so people can understand what you're talking about. In my humble opinion, your writing style is an extension of you, and if I buy your book I want to get a feel for you through your words – not get the impression the text has been written by a committee of copy editors.

So however much you may feel you need to brush up on your writing skills, by all means do so – but don't let it consume everything else. That's where good writing coaches can be extremely helpful, because very quickly they can judge just how much polishing your writing skills really need without destroying your uniqueness. With the best will in the world courses can only cater for common denominators. Coaches, on the other hand, tailor their activities to your individual needs which to me seems much more cost-effective. See Chapter 17 for some recommendations.

Co-Authors

I have the experience of working with a co-author on two of my books. In both cases we split the proceeds 50-50, and I believe that's customary when both co-authors contribute equal amounts to the project. This issue can be a tricky one if you don't know what to watch out for, especially as people are likely to have differing views on what constitutes 50% of the effort.

One expert and one (topic-literate) writer

In the first case, on "The Jewellery Book," I worked with a jeweller/gemmologist. That turned out well because our skills and input were complementary. He provided all the technical content and I did all the writing, which was a reasonable 50-50 split. We worked to a very detailed chapter structure, and would sit down with a tape recorder once a week or so. During each session I would "interview" my co-author in accordance with the structure and so obtain the technical material needed. After he had gone home I would then write up the chapter concerned, which he and I would then edit as needed. No problems.

Two experts (who also happened to be writers!)

The second co-authored book (my fourth) was "Writing Words That Sell." Although it was my concept and structure, the content was written jointly with a US colleague who at the time worked in almost exactly the same fields as I do. On reflection this was not a good idea, as we were equally qualified to write most chapters – perhaps a case of too many experts and certainly, too much crossover. We carved the chapters up more or less 50-50 and shared them out, but of course with two professional writers producing material inevitably there were differences in style and approach.

In the end I took over editorship of the co-author's work and re-aligned his material so that it more closely matched the style of the book, although I didn't change his content. He didn't mind my doing this but it was a lot of extra work for me.

In my experience, then, co-authorship works well when there is a rapport between the authors BUT each one supplies a different/complementary skill set. When both authors do similar things and can virtually replace each other, however, it doesn't necessarily work out quite so well.

Ghostwriters

If you really can't face the prospect of writing a book yourself, there is always the option to hire someone to do it for you. Good ghostwriters charge a lot of money for doing the job, and quite rightly – it usually represents weeks or months of extremely hard work.

If you find someone willing to ghostwrite a book for you cheaply, be careful because they may not be very good. A bad ghostwriter still costs money but in the end you have to do most of it yourself or hand over an inferior manuscript to be edited by your publisher. If you're self-publishing you may need to hire a freelance editor to sort out the mess or worse still, not be aware that the text is awful and publish it unedited.

Some ghostwriters will charge a little less if their name appears on the book. Variants of this concept are:

- by (Your Name) and (Ghostwriter's Name)
- by (Your Name) with (Ghostwriter's Name)

Sometimes the ghostwriter will accept a combination consisting, perhaps, of a lower fee and a percentage of your royalties. Also the ghostwriter may want a credit on the book as "edited by..." It's all down to negotiation, really.

Ghostwriters aren't all that easy to find. Because people who use ghostwriters don't normally want anyone else to know they've used one, ghostwriters' wares do not tend to get advertised widely. Probably the best way to find one is to ask your publishers, if you have gone that route, or if you're self-publishing contact a self-publishing or author services company and ask them.

You can also run a search on the web, of course, but check the person's credentials before you contact them. Then invest some quality time in getting to know them. Good chemistry is very important if you're going to work this closely with someone.

The people who use ghostwriters are not necessarily bad at writing. Many are very good at writing but because they have other more important tasks to deal with (e.g. running major corporations, governments, etc) they simply don't have time to write their own stuff. In these cases it makes economical sense to pay someone else to do it, even if they do charge a lot of money.

How you work with a ghostwriter, again, varies enormously according to their methods and your availability. What is true universally, though, is that you will need to allocate quite a lot of time to work with the ghostwriter, even though that is far less than you would need to write the book yourself.

Often ghostwriters are journalists and because of their training they can do a lot of research and background assembly of material for you. But usually what makes a book interesting is the "author's" own spin on the subject matter. And no matter how good the ghostwriter is s/he is not psychic and cannot become you. You need to provide them with the raw material they need to craft your book, and be generous with it.

Suzan St Maur

CHAPTER 6

Planning Your Book

If you're going to submit proposals you'll need to plan your book sooner rather than later – good discipline for you although you can modify the structure later on as you work through the manuscript. Even if you're self-publishing, it makes a lot of sense to plan your book very thoroughly before you start writing. Just as you would with a house-building project or new business, you will benefit greatly from planning your book carefully because a) it will make it easier for you to write up the final manuscript and b) it will make it a better book.

Why So Many Books Get Started But Not Finished

How many people do you know, or have you heard of, who have started a book but not been able to finish it? That old cliché about the "unfinished novel in a drawer?" (Both fiction and nonfiction come into the story here.)

I know the answer to that one because I have fallen victim to it myself. Here's a painful truth:

You'll only ever finish a book – fiction or nonfiction – if you've planned and structured the whole thing properly beforehand.

I'm sure there will be fiction authors who laugh at me and talk about how they just develop a few strong characters and then let them define a plot as the story progresses. Now I'm going to put my head on the block and say, bullshit. You can start a book

37

without a proper structure and planning, but I'll put money on the fact that very few of those books ever get finished.

Structure Is Critical

Before you do anything else, carve this important motto into your work:

> *"I will structure my book according to what my readers need to know, in the order they need to know it. That will take priority at all times over what I think I should say."*

I know that might sound a bit juvenile but if you have read as many nonfiction/"how to" books as I have, you will begin to understand what I mean.

Your book is not an opportunity to let it all hang out, as they used to say in the 1970s. It's an opportunity to share your knowledge provided that it is presented in a way that will benefit readers.

The Right Order

With some topics – like writing a book, i.e. this book – the order in which you organise your material pretty well suggests itself, i.e. a chronology or timeline where you start at the beginning of the process and finish at the end of it. Here, I've started with your book as a gleam in your eye and worked through the process of devising it, creating proposals for a publisher, and then getting it written in full, although in real life you'll probably find that some of the steps involved overlap or occur in a slightly different order.

With my books on weddings, in the main I have used the chronology of how to organise a wedding as a skeleton structure. In "How To Get Married In Green" (about eco-friendly weddings) I began with a chapter on jewellery, on the basis of getting engaged being the first step in the process!

There are other ways to order your material, too, and many of those suggest themselves in the same way. A book about gardening, for example, can be ordered in one of several ways depending on your particular slant on the subject:

1. Calendar – month-by-month
2. Types – annuals, perennials, shrubs, herbaceous, etc
3. Species – various flowering shrubs, roses, azaleas, heathers, etc
4. Vegetables according to season of planting and ripening/fruiting
5. Planting and designs for different types and sizes of garden
6. Garden styles – cottage, formal, modern, container, etc
7. ...and so-on.

Another approach to ordering your material is the encyclopaedic route. Depending on your topic not only is this a very easy way to slot together a large number of sub-topics that don't necessarily form part of a step-by-step process, but also it's a very easy way for your readers to find the information they want most. I've used this in two of my books so far – "The A to Z of Video and TV Jargon" and "The A to Z of Wedding Worries and how to put them right" – both of which titles are more or less self-explanatory.

Don't Skip The Details

Whatever way of ordering your material you choose, you'll do yourself a favour in the long run by going into quite a lot of detail, even at this early stage.

Apart from the reader benefits, the more detailed your structure the easier it will be for you to write the final manuscript. Spend a good chunk of time planning your chapters and ensuring they run in the right order. Subdivide the chapters down into bullet point structure of their own and flesh that out as far as you can. Then, before you go any further, think about research.

If you know all there is to know about your topic then that's fine. But don't try to incorporate your knowledge directly into draft text of the book. There needs to be at least one degree of separation between your raw knowledge and how you put it across to your readers.

Because your structure must be developed on the basis of what elements of your expertise your readers need to know, your knowledge outpouring must be tempered by the discipline of a reader-friendly order. Whenever you find yourself floundering a bit, think of your reader and imagine you're talking to him or her over a cup of coffee. What would s/he want to find out, and in what order?

Research: How To Go About It

The first port of call in any nonfiction book's research journey must always be the book's readers. By knowing these people well and understanding their issues and problems, you may even find that the book's structure and content suggest themselves. So how do you go about it?

There's no great mystique to it. If you want to get to know your readers, go and talk to them. That's what I do. But I don't always follow the most obvious route.

Of course a lot of your research into your readers can, in theory, be done at your desk. You can use your common sense to work out the fact that the readership of a book about weddings is likely to be predominantly female, mostly within the 20 – 40 age group with a secondary audience of brides' mothers, with a reasonable amount of money to spend but not enough to justify hiring a wedding planner, etc. In the same way you can work out that a book about how to write your own advertising and PR material will appeal to people in small businesses – sole traders and the lower end of SMEs – trying to maximize small marketing budgets, with a secondary audience of people in departments of larger companies who, once again, are trying to maximize ad budgets squeezed by a current financial cutback or recession.

However, quality of information is important here. Even small nuances can make a huge difference to your understanding of your readership. And one thing common sense doesn't achieve, is to uncover issues and problems that no-one likes to talk about. Yet often it's precisely these issues and problems that your own expertise can help solve, so making your book even more valuable to its readers.

One time I was asked to produce a series of audio tapes to inform and motivate a team of mobile automotive technicians working for one of the UK's leading "motoring organisations." From the information I was given and found out from my desk I knew that they were all rather independent individuals, many of them working pretty remote territories all over the UK in their vans and only meeting with their colleagues and superiors on fairly rare occasions. They were key customer-facing staff, of course, because they were the people customers met when their cars had broken down. They were perceived by customers to be knights in shining armour and as a result, many had quite lively egos. Great, all good stuff, and easy to discover through the comfortable media of telephone, fax and e-mail. And that might have been enough for some writers.

But Suze's nose kept twitching. The picture looked too rosy, too settled. I needed to know if anything smelly was lurking under the floorboards. My client, a senior HR manager, through no fault of his own hardly ever got to leave Head Office and never had the chance to see our target audience in action. It was possible there were problems he didn't know about.

So, not quite donning a wig and a false nose but certainly keeping a low profile, I sneaked (having got permission from my client of course) into a rare regional convention of these people in another city. Boring old stuff from the podium and very interesting quips from members of the audience to one another in the back rows of the hall (where of course I was sitting.) I detect unhappy noises and make notes. Next stop, out on the road.

It just so happens that an old friend of mine owns a big service station and car workshop near where I live and his place is a certified depot for "motoring organisations." I learned that most local technicians in the "motoring organisation" business hang out in these certified depots because that's where they bring in customers' cars for more complex repair. Over some vile machine-brewed coffee late one night Suze was shooting the breeze with representatives not only from the clients' company but also from their two key competitors. And guess what? In casual conversation it turned out that my clients' company was being ridiculed by its competitors because of a variety of issues, several of which my poor client knew nothing whatsoever about.

So, what difference did that make to the project I was working on, and my knowledge of the audience – in this case several hundred people like the poor man who was lambasted by the competitors' staff over a cup of revolting coffee in that depot? Actually, it was like watching dominoes fall over. By end of business the following day my client's company had launched an urgent investigation into the whole thing. By the end of that week they had discovered that the same problems were widespread, across the country. By the beginning of the next week our entire communications project had been changed to accommodate the new findings. We then went ahead with the revised approach and it worked. I shudder to think how much money my client's company would have wasted on expensive, pointless videos and printed materials had we not uncovered those issues in time.

There's a lot to be said for using these "mystery shopper" techniques to research and get to know your audience. Although some people might say it's dishonest to conceal your identity, the problem is people won't always be honest with you if you tell them who you really are and why you're asking these questions. That's especially true of rank-and-file staff in large organisations, if they think you're "management." Many will tell you what they think you want to hear. Similarly consumers in stores and shopping malls will put up barriers, especially if you're walking around with a video camera crew or even an audio recorder. Even the people brought into "focus groups" (those supposedly informal discussion sessions highly revered by researchers and marketing people) tend to exaggerate their existing opinions and invent an opinion on the spot if they didn't happen to have one previously. The reason in all cases, I believe, is because people find these circumstances artificial and intimidating - hardly conducive to relaxed, natural dialogue.

You're far more likely to get the truth from staff in a large organisation, say, if they think you're the person who's come in to fix the photocopying machine, or from shoppers if you're pushing a loaded cart in a supermarket and strike up a conversation with them while waiting to go through the checkout.

However even if you're upfront and say you're researching for a book, you can still get to the truth by gaining people's confidence, and that you do by becoming their friend. How do you befriend your interviewees? You get them to talk about themselves. And not just their business or professional selves, either, but their personal selves. Pick up on some small thing to get the conversation going... a golf trophy on a shelf, a picture of some children or pets, an attractive piece of jewellery, the quality of the coffee, the weather. Sometimes you'll find that their demeanour changes abruptly – they soften, smile, relax. Once you've got them going on that, ask their opinion on a small point that's relevant to your book project. Then gradually guide the conversation into everything else you want to know.

There are very few people in the industrialised world who positively will not warm to someone whom they believe is genuinely interested in them, their life, and their opinions. Over the years I've conducted literally thousands of corporate interviews, many of which were recorded on video or audio, and in all that time I only failed to get through to two people. One was a 7-foot car factory worker with tattoos everywhere, a small chain through one nostril, and a severe speech impediment. The other was a rock band's road manager who was about to get fried by the electrics in pouring rain on an open-air stage surrounded by live cables. Everybody else, though, eventually opened up and spoke their thoughts freely.

It's not because I've got a friendly face, large cleavage, bulging wallet or anything else. It's because I genuinely like people and I am genuinely interested in them. Members of your audience aren't idiots. If you're only pretending to be interested in them, they'll know. So you have to *be* interested. Really. And if you are, you'll get the results you want.

Once you get the conversation rolling you need to employ some of the basic techniques used by good corporate/business TV interviewers (not journalists and TV interviewers, as their interviews are usually adversarial – makes for more exciting TV, they say.)

- You probably won't need to base your questions on the news reporters' list of "who, what, where, when, how and why," because you're more likely to be looking for feelings and inclinations rather than hard facts. But even though you don't ask your questions in the news reporter's style, that list can be a useful structure for you to base your thinking on.

- Be careful how you phrase your questions – be tactful and polite.

- Always make your questions open-ended, so they invite an answer. Ask for opinions. People love to give their opinions.

- Never ask a "closed" question (one that can be answered with a "yes" or a "no.") Use "open" questions with the news reporters' list as a basis, but be gentle – not just "why does everyone hate bindweed so much," but "why do you think bindweed has become such a problem for gardeners?"

- When asking a question, just ask one – don't include more than one key thought.

- When you've asked a question, shut up. Let the person speak. Don't interrupt or attempt to steer what they're saying.

- If they falter or hesitate on an important point, don't press them on it. Ask them something else, then return to your original point later on, remembering to ask the question in a different way so they don't realise it's the same point. You'll be surprised how well that can work.

- And when you've finished, thank them. They've helped you to plan your book better and more effectively.

Desk Research

I've gone into quite a lot of what's relevant here in Chapter 3, so I won't repeat myself   about using Google and its various tools, plus collecting paper-based cuttings, etc.

The other type of desk research many of us use, is reading other people's books on related topics. Be warned, however, that lifting information from someone else's book is not only immoral but also can get you into pretty deep doo-doo, legally speaking. Plagiarism, although technically not the same as copyright infringement, actually amounts to much the same thing and by trying to pass someone else's work off as your own, even if you were to get away without a lawsuit, would be very damaging to your credibility as an author.

Needless to say the advent of the internet has made plagiarism almost into an international sport, to the extent that you can now employ tracking services and software to find out who is passing off your work as their own anywhere in the world. The ease with which people can cut and paste text has meant that the old tricks of students using someone else's essay material has become as easy as a few clicks. This need not concern you unless your book is of an academic nature, but be warned. Not only will you have to avoid using anyone else's material, but also if your book gets published online or as an eBook, you may find others helping themselves to yours.

If you do want to include some quotations from others' books or articles, even very long ones, doing so normally isn't difficult, although it can be time consuming to track down an author or copyright owner. As you'll see later in this book I have quoted from a wonderful book by Rachael Stock, "The Insider's Guide To Getting Your Book Published," and all it took to gain her permission was a request and a promise to give her book the appropriate credits. Having bits of your book quoted in other books is good publicity and not many authors will turn you down, provided you behave respectfully and honourably.

CHAPTER 7

Your Publishing Choices

Today there are two basic publishing "pathways" - self-publishing and its variants (some good, some not so good) and conventional publishing by an external publisher which I go into in Chapter 8.

The Howlers

However let's start with the choice nearly everyone has heard about – and laughed at: the "vanity publisher." Essentially they flatter you into parting with a large sum of money in exchange for which they "publish" your book. Because usually they're glorified jobbing printers they put your text straight out as it comes in with no editing or checking, print it up, bind the books and deliver them to you in boxes, leaving you to do whatever you want with them. Promises of marketing and distribution are seldom fulfilled. Needless to say this is an expensive and usually disappointing way to publish your book, unless you're not short of cash and want an ego-trip.

The latest incarnation of vanity publishing is particularly clever, and downright cruel to newbie authors who have a treasured novel in a drawer. Just for fun I investigated one of these publishers and to all intents and purposes, the initial phases of negotiation were just as you would expect from a conventional publisher. I had to submit proposals with three sample chapters; after several weeks I received an email from them saying that they were now passing my proposals on to their chief editor.

Another few weeks and I got a letter saying that the chief editor believed my stuff showed promise although I would have to do more work on the book, that I would be expected to make a "small contribution" towards the cost of the book's production, and please would I telephone her to discuss this in more detail.

I had smelled a rat some time before, but the "small contribution" really set the alarm off. I dialled the number and the phone was answered by a woman with a growling voice like an 80-year-old pipe smoker… "yes, this is she." We skittered around the subject for a few minutes and eventually I thought, let's not waste any more time here, so asked what she meant by the "small contribution."

"Well of course, as publishers we invest at least £10,000 pounds in producing a new book and getting it out to the markets," she rumbled, "and all we would ask from you is just £2,600." That was for a print run of a few thousand paperback copies…

What really irked me about this obvious vanity publishing scam was the way that they used conventional publishing techniques at first, to get me on the hook. Less cynical authors could well find the early part of the process really gratifying – "oh, at long last someone thinks my book is good enough to publish" – and once they eventually get to the crunch point where money changes hands, they're emotionally too committed to the project to back out.

Needless to say I had no hesitation in backing out, and took pleasure in telling the old foghorn what I thought of her business practice.

Hybrids

In addition there are a few hybrid options available whereby you pay towards the cost of producing your book, but the company concerned acts as an umbrella "publishing house" and helps to distribute and list your book. Sometimes the deal offered is that you agree to buy a number of your own books at author's discount, either to sell on yourself or to give away as promotional pieces. Although I know that there are some good, genuine businesses running out there, I'm still a little nervous of some of these hybrids because I believe there's a risk of falling between two stools – it costs you to use them, but you don't have the freedom to distribute the book yourself and their marketing efforts can vary from very good to useless.

Publishing Services

There are also publishing organisations which offer services to self-publishers on a menu basis. This can include anything from print and production only, up to everything starting with advice on writing the book, editing, design and layout, etc., right through to the finished books in boxes. This can be useful for self-publishers.

Then, there is a delightful company called Bookshaker... who just happen to have published this book! Not only are the founders great friends of mine but also they are colleagues whose talents and achievements I respect very much. Essentially, they've managed to put together publishing options that allow you many of the advantages of conventional publishing and ePublishing, and you take home a far higher percentage in royalties. Here follows a short piece by Joe Gregory of Bookshaker, explaining how it works…

Bookshaker: A Different Approach

By Joe Gregory

This is our own publishing company. It has a number of imprints including Lean Marketing Press, Publishing Academy, NativeSpain and BookShaker, and at the time of writing (November 2009) has published almost 80 nonfiction titles since 2003. Although we're very much like mainstream publishers in some ways (especially in that we can afford to be picky) there are certain benefits (and certain limitations) to our offer too.

Take a look at the following information and if you're interested then get in touch with us at www.bookshaker.com/authors

The Deal

Royalty: 20%-50% Net (based on author's platform, completeness, sales achieved).

Term: 5 Years.

Process: POD (Print on Demand), goes to Lithographic print when/if certain conditions are met.

Distribution: Ingram, Gardners, Online/Offline (USA, UK, Europe and Canada) plus ebooks distributed through OverDrive (much better than you'd get with LightningSource alone) and Smashwords.

The Benefits

- You get much higher starting royalties and as your book sales increase so will your royalty, so there's a genuine reason for you to want to promote your book.

- We provide free access to all of our Publishing Academy courses as well as free access to the Publishing Academy member's area. This gives you far more good advice on promoting yourself and your book than you'll get anywhere else.
- We do lots of active promotion on behalf of our authors.
- We grant you a licence to sell the PDF version of your book direct and keep 100% of the profit.
- We'll set you up with a blog (that you will own) to act as a marketing focus for your book, fans and followers.
- By streamlining the publishing process we can get your manuscript edited, typeset, packaged and to print within 6-8 weeks (this is better than any mainstream publisher that we know of, typically 18-24 months and even better than the vanity presses, who charge you and still take 3-6 months to get your book done).
- We pay quarterly royalties.
- We provide author's copies at print cost + £2.50 so where we make a profit is transparent and easy to identify.

The Downsides

- We only take nonfiction and since we started, our acceptance rate has averaged about 7%. So make sure you've done your homework before submitting proposals.
- We don't pay advances. This is a throwback to a previous era and is a wasteful practice in our opinion. We believe money should be earned and we view the process as a partnership.
- We won't give retailers the option to return or destroy books. For this reason your book is less likely to be out on their shelves than it would be with a traditional mainstream, even though it's available for retailers to order.

- We'd prefer to pay the author a decent amount of the profit from their book. This means we only offer 35% standard trade discount and expect certain minimum requirements to be met before we'll increase this for bookstores.
- We're small and relatively unknown compared to the publishing giants, so we may not meet your need for external approval in the form of landing a big, posh publishing deal.
- We don't take on resource-needy authors, so if you're not planning to do your bit to promote your book you'll quickly find our support will be less forthcoming. We help those who are willing to help themselves.

Bookshaker publish other titles via the Publishing Academy website, covering the whole publishing and business element of producing nonfiction books – see Further Reading.

Self-Publishing

As I've already suggested, self-publishing must never be confused with the old-fashioned "vanity publishing." As I outlined above, the latter is usually carried out by unscrupulous companies who charge you a fortune to produce a few hundred copies of your book so you can bask in the glory of seeing your name in print.

Self-publishing, in the appropriate circumstances, is simply a cost-effective way of doing the business.

As the nuts-and-bolts elements of book production become cheaper and cheaper through the advancement of technology, self-publishing becomes increasingly attractive for some nonfiction book writers, depending on circumstances. With modern print-on-demand (POD) facilities, too, you avoid the need to have hundreds or thousands of copies printed initially just to keep the unit cost down. Now you can have a handful of books printed at a time and still keep the unit cost within reason.

The advantages of self-publishing (as I see them) are:

- You do not have to answer to anyone else on design, content, editing, etc

- You do not have to spend any time on finding or convincing a publisher to take your book on

- You get to keep all profit from book sales

The disadvantages of self-publishing (as I see them) are:

- You have to find the money to get the book produced

- You can get editorial and design support, but you have to pay for it

- You have to organise and pay for distribution of your book

- You will not find it easy to get your book on to Amazon and into other key distribution channels

- You have to run a publishing business as well as whatever else you do

Essentially if you want to run a small publishing business and you have the contacts and wherewithal to secure good distribution, you'll do well with self-publishing. This is especially relevant if you are a speaker, lecturer, or live performer, where you will have captive audiences to whom to sell signed copies of your book.

If you prefer just to write and promote your book without the other headaches or you don't have the opportunity to distribute the book effectively, you'll find you sleep better at night if you can get your book published conventionally, or by Bookshaker.

In any case you'll find a goldmine of information about the business and marketing side of publishing nonfiction books in some of Bookshaker's other titles – especially "The Wealthy Author" by Joe Gregory and Debbie Jenkins.

See Chapter 17 for details.

CHAPTER 8

The Conventional Publisher Route

Just to avoid any confusion, what I mean here is that you submit proposals for your book to an established print book publisher (like HarperCollins, Macmillan, Pearson, etc) and if they like it, they will publish it. You do not have to put your hand in your pocket at any point of the process, which is the key differentiator between this and self-publishing.

The advantages of getting your book published externally by a conventional publisher are:

- It gives your book status (less so than in the past, but still good if it's a well known, respected publisher)

- Your book will be distributed to all the agreed markets at no cost to you

- They will handle and pay for all design, setup, print and production costs

- You'll probably get paid a small advance on royalties

The disadvantages are:

- They will be in the driving seat, although they will listen to what you want to do

- They will say that they'll market the book, but they won't (more on that later)

- You will need to negotiate your contract with them very carefully

- The percentage of each sale you receive will be far less than if you self-publish

- You won't see any income from the book's sales until your royalties have paid off any advance you've been given

- It probably will take quite a long time for the book to come out, after you submit the final manuscript

How To Find The Right Publishers

The entire book publishing industry is driven by something called "lists." Every conventional book publisher has one or more of these things. Essentially a list is a genre of book – e.g. business books (often subdivided into marketing, finance, management, etc)... self-help books (Hodder & Stoughton's Teach Yourself series is a good example)... cookery books... lifestyle books (DIY and home improvement, Feng Shui, flower arranging)... biographies and autobiographies... and so-on.

Fiction publishers have especially well defined lists, e.g.... romantic... literary... historical... science... science fantasy... erotica... you name it.

Lists are also useful devices for publishers to hide behind when rejecting a new book proposal, as in "your concept does not fit in with our list." It's probably unfair to say that if your book concept doesn't fit into any known publisher's list it will never get published. If your idea is good enough, it might. But if you can slot your book concept into a known genre – a list – you'll find that publishers look upon it more favourably. This is especially true of fiction, but it applies to nonfiction too.

Anyway like them or not we must be driven by these lists, if we're to get our books published by the corporate listers. So, we have to research which publisher does what list, and match our book concept to publishers in whose list we feel it will fit.

Assuming the general area covered by your book is one which is fairly well established, it's easy to find other books on similar topics in online bookstores like Amazon. Usually on a book's Amazon listing page it will say who the publisher is. You then run a search on that publisher's name and get through to their website.

Alternatively you can run a Google (or similar) search using appropriate keywords. I might use something like this:

> "book publishers" + "business books"
> + marketing + writing

...but you're probably far better at choosing effective key words than I am!

If you prefer the offline mode, the best book I have ever found in the UK is "Writers' and Artists' Yearbook." This is published every year and contains listings of most publishers in the UK, plus the better known publishers in the USA, Australia, Canada, New Zealand, Ireland and South Africa. It also contains every other imaginable resource a writer might need. It's published by A&C Black (Publishers) Ltd., and the ISBN is 0713669365. The book is widely available from bookshops, public libraries and online bookstores.

If you live outside the UK, you'll find that most of the major English language markets will have a similar book of their own. You'll find them in public libraries, bookshops and online. I've listed a few in chapter 17, but I'm sure there are many more to choose from, especially in the USA.

It will take you a while to plod through the publishers listed in directories like these as they're categorised alphabetically and you need to read the small print to get the descriptions of the publishers' lists. Also be warned. In the case of the UK's "Writers' and Artists' Year Book" I've found that the descriptions are not always very accurate and often the staff members listed have moved on by the time you approach them. If you find some publishers in there that seem likely candidates for your book, it's best to telephone or look them up on the internet to find out more before you approach them.

You'll find now that most publishers have websites and many of those sites have a section devoted to "wannabe" authors, usually under the heading of "authors" or "submissions." In those sections you'll probably find guidelines on the sort of new books they're interested in and also what they want to see in any new book submission. This is well worth taking seriously as it can cut through a lot of tedious doo-doo and save you weeks of work and waiting time.

Some even give you the option to submit your preliminary book proposal online, which is great! I submitted the initial proposals for Powerwriting to Prentice Hall Business via their website and I ended up with an offer from them for it (which I accepted). More about how to create proposals and submit them in Chapter 9.

Literary Agents

I have had literary agents in the past but nowadays very few are interested in taking on unknown nonfiction authors, for good reason. If you have read the foregoing you'll know that business books and many other nonfiction works don't always make a great deal of money. So you're only worth ten percent of not very much to an agent – i.e. not worth bothering about.

In any case now that it's so much easier to find the right publishers for your kind of book you don't really need an agent unless you're writing fiction. Even when I had an agent I used to find that I did the face-to-face selling job to the publisher a lot better than she did. Initially it was helpful to get them to negotiate the contracts, but now that I've done quite a few by myself I've worked out what to watch out for (more on that later).

Also, with more and more publishers having websites and inviting new book submissions direct, I would hazard a guess that they prefer to deal direct with authors. Although there still is some "old school tie" business being done in publishing/literary agents' circles, it is dying out. And with that, so are the advantages you might have gained for your book in the past by having your agent sell it to an editor she was at college with, or over a glass of warm white wine at a book fair.

If you're doing nonfiction my advice is, don't waste time looking for an agent. Go straight for a publisher. With some background knowledge like this book and perhaps some advice from a lawyer – or from Rachael Stock's book, "The Insider's Guide To Getting Your Book

Published" – to check your publishing contract, you'll do just as well and keep the ten percent for yourself.

And the last word on agents: beware those who ask you to pay them to represent you, unless it is a very small amount to cover admin expenses. Paying an agent is like paying a vanity publisher – an expensive luxury that usually leads to nothing.

How To Approach Your Chosen Publishers

First of all, don't make the mistake of thinking you need to write the whole book before you find a publisher. That's usually (but not always) true of fiction. However with nonfiction you don't need to write it all in order to get an offer from a publisher – they can tell whether to run with it or not on the basis of a detailed proposal. And in many ways I think it's better not to write more than an outline first anyway. That's because you're likely to enter into discussions with the publisher about fine-tuning and re-aligning content before you finalise the deal. If you have already written the book it may mean that some of your time has been wasted.

Another issue is that, supposedly, etiquette says you must not submit your book proposal to more than one publisher simultaneously. I know some authors still stick to that principle but I'm afraid I look upon it as a business deal, which means offering it to more than one potential "customer" at a time if that's appropriate. I honestly don't think publishers are precious about it anymore, except perhaps in the case of literary fiction which still has a terribly genteel aura surrounding it. So my advice would be, submit your proposals to whoever you want, when you want to.

CHAPTER 9

Submitting Proposals

If you can find out what your chosen publisher's submission guidelines are then all you do is follow those exactly. However, many publishers do not specify what they like to receive, so you should follow the following conventional approach...

Submitting A Book Concept

If you're going into a publisher cold, you're best to start with a covering letter addressed to the correct person – usually the editor in charge of the "list" you've aimed your book at. To find out the name, phone the publisher's switchboard and ask. Then keep the letter very short, and don't grovel or be apologetic in any way. Just be politely assertive and say something like this...

Dear (Mr/Ms NAME)

You may find it useful to see the attached outline concept for "(TITLE OF BOOK)"

I hope you'll agree that it could provide a valid contribution to your (Whatever) list.

Please be kind enough to let me know if you would like to see more detailed proposals.

I look forward to hearing from you.

Yours sincerely...

Enclose with the letter a one-sheet on which you describe the essence of the book – I've included a sample of style and length in the appendices.

Needless to say it has to be absolutely riveting. It also must have two or three lines saying who you are and why you are qualified to write the book. Then add in an SAE and send the package off.

Although you may be able to get hold of the editor's email address, I wouldn't approach them electronically unless they make it very clear that they welcome email inquiries. The good news is that nowadays some editors actually prefer to receive initial enquiries by email as it's simpler to deal with and reply to, but don't count on it. There are still many rather old-fashioned editors in the publishing industry...

However if you do send in a paper enquiry, be sure to include your email address on the letter and one-sheet so they can respond to you that way if they want to.

Finally, if you want to be on the safe side, you can include the international copyright sign alongside (to the left of) your name and the year in which you're submitting the work, like this:

© Your Name 20XX

If the document is likely to cross over into the next year, it's advisable to include that year too:

© Your Name 20XX-20XY

Don't be too keen to slap copyright signs all over your work though. The fact that you have written your work up and declared yourself as the author is just as much of a safeguard of your copyright as the symbol is, and some publishers might feel their professionalism is being offended by it... you shouldn't even suspect that they would abuse your copyright! What I normally do is place one copyright symbol, in a small font size, somewhere fairly discreet at the beginning or end of the one-sheet. It makes me feel a bit happier (after my experiences of ideas theft, see Chapter 3) but it doesn't shove my suspicious nature up the editor's nose.

Main Elements Of Proposals

In the absence of guidance from the publisher, here are the main elements of detailed proposals that you will be expected to include. I've taken these from the proposals I did for Powerwriting which I have included in full in the appendices. The elements were set out by Prentice Hall but are typical of all the publishers' submission guidelines that I've seen.

- **Synopsis**... the "elevator speech" about the book (probably taken from your one-sheet)
- **Competition**... what other books on the subject exist and why yours is better
- **Market/audience**... to whom the book will appeal and why
- **International market**... if the book is suitable for translation
- **Style and approach**... informal or formal, textbook or friendly advice, didactic or anecdotal, etc
- **Endorsements**... whether you could get a suitable famous person to write a foreword, etc
- **Delivery information**... anticipated length of book, anticipated time required to complete, etc
- **The author**... brief biography, including any earlier books you have written or contributed to
- **The background to the book**... why and how you came to devise it
- **Chapter list**... preferably with a title and as many bullet-pointed details as possible of each one
- **Sample chapter or excerpts**... 1,000 words or so to demonstrate style and approach

Have a look at the example I include in the appendix, as that will give you an idea of how to approach doing yours. Don't be afraid to be informal, as I always am! If you keep your style simple, direct and enjoyable to read you will earn brownie points from the editor, believe me. Usually book proposals are very dry and tedious so if yours are pleasant to read it can do you nothing but good.

You'll find sample book proposals in the appendices.

CHAPTER 10

The Formal Offer

Once you have submitted your detailed proposals you may have to wait quite a while – several weeks – before you hear anything. If, after a couple of months, you haven't heard it's reasonable to phone or write to the publisher and ask if they received your proposal safely and if there's any further information they would like at this stage. But that's all. It's never wise to rush them and they will get back to you eventually. Book publishing moves at a far slower pace than most other industries – (aren't they lucky?)

When you do hear, they may come back with a number of questions plus suggestions for improvements and changes to the content of your book. You can take it that although they will listen to your arguments and may concede a few points, generally speaking if you want them to publish your book, you play ball and do as they ask.

Once all the tweaks and edits are done, the publisher should come back with a formal offer, saying, "Yes, we want to publish your book." Usually at this point they will say how much they are prepared to pay as an advance on royalties, if they do that. Alternatively they may send you a draft contract outlining all aspects of the deal they are offering you.

Many more modern publishers – Bookshaker included – don't bother with an advance on royalties which is OK, because it means although you finance yourself while writing the book, you start earning as soon as it starts selling. If you are offered an advance, unless you're Jackie Collins or J K Rowling it won't pay anything like enough to cover the time you spend writing your book. That's an investment you must be prepared to make yourself. Advances are normally paid in 2 or 3 chunks with payment points at signing of the contract, delivery of the manuscript, and publication.

As a guideline, I got four formal offers on Powerwriting ranging from GBP £500 (USD $800) to GBP £4,000 (USD $6,400.) No prizes for guessing which I took, but in fact the money was not the only reason – Prentice Hall also offered the best distribution worldwide. GBP £4,000 is considered quite a large advance for a business book by an author who isn't famous (i.e. not Richard Branson or Bill Gates) – but the fact that I have had a few earlier business books published did help to raise the ante.

In some cases, authors will be offered a deal whereby they write the book for a fee. In fairness this is far more likely to happen if the publishers commission the book project themselves and then select an author to write it for them, but it's worth mentioning anyway.

The most usual offer is of an advance, followed by royalties. From here, let me hand you over to Rachael Stock – a very successful and well known publisher and editor – whose excellent book, "The Insider's Guide To Getting Your Book Published," is well worth reading. Rachael has kindly allowed me to quote excerpts from her book here. My leader dots (...) indicate where I have moved on in Rachael's text – I didn't think she would be too impressed if I typed out her entire book!

...the royalty is the amount of money you receive per book sold. The royalty is a percentage of either the recommended retail price (the price printed on the book cover), or a percentage of the 'net receipts' (normally calculated as the cover price of the book, minus whatever the bookseller takes as their cut). By 'the bookseller' we might mean just the actual bookstore itself, for larger publishers who sell direct, or we might mean the bookstore and the distributor.

...Royalty on net receipts

This is widespread for many nonfiction publishers, especially educational or academic publishers and illustrated publishers/packagers, but not exclusively. It means you get a percentage of whatever amount the publisher gets for the book from the bookseller. So for example if the cover price of the book is £10 and the bookseller buys the book from the publisher and 50 percent discount, then the net receipt on which the royalty is calculated will be £5. The royalty rate for net receipts contracts should be higher than the royalty rate for published price contracts, so that the actual amount the author receives is roughly the same.

...Flat or escalating royalty

Whether you get a contract based on published price or net receipts, it is fairly common to get an escalating royalty so that the more copies of the book are sold, the higher the percentage of the royalty you get.

...Advance

...Advances are normally paid in two or three instalments. The first part is paid on signature of contract, then you may get a second part on delivery and acceptance of the manuscript and/or a second or third part on publication of the book.

Suzan St Maur

CHAPTER 11

Publishing Contracts

Until you sign a contract you're not under any obligation to proceed, even though you may have accepted the publisher's offer. I have included a sample publishing contract as an appendix to give you an idea of what it looks like but in the meantime here are the main areas you need to look out for.

First of all, some key tips in the form of excerpts from the chapter entitled "Negotiating a contract," from Rachael Stock's excellent book, "The Insider's Guide To Getting Your Book Published."

...A really core principle is: never, ever be afraid to ask what something means. If a publisher won't tell you in words you understand, then ask again. A good publisher will always be able and willing to explain the financial terms and contract clauses to you.

The second core principle is: if you are going to negotiate, be nice but quietly determined and always look for a win-win. As with any kind of negotiation, if you can reach a point where both parties think they have won, it's the best kind of outcome you could possibly have.

The third core principle is: where there are lots of variables, decided which you care about and which you are less worried about so you can give on others but stick on some.

> **...Golden rule**
> Contracts work both ways. They are there to set out the obligations and responsibilities of both author and publisher. A good contract will protect you as well as protecting the publisher.
>
> **...Golden rule**
> A good contract will ensure that if the book goes out of print, all rights revert to you.
>
> **...Golden rule**
> Think very hard about what rights you think the publisher should have and what you want to keep.
>
> **...Golden rule**
> Always make sure you understand your obligations under the contract, and that you are happy with the publisher's obligations too.

If you are going the conventional publishing route I really would urge you to read Rachael's book. It's brilliant, and I only wish I could have read that before I started out as an author.

For what it's worth, here are some of my own tips based on experience learned the hard way!

Rights

Be sure that if the publisher wants the electronic rights they intend to do something with them. Some publishers seem just to hang on to the e-rights with no intention of developing an eBook or anything else along those lines. I wonder if they don't try this on purely to stop you issuing the material as an eBook which might affect sales of the printed version. Anyway, you should get a clear understanding with them about the electronic rights, and the fact that you should retain them if the publisher can't specify what they will do with them. The further we get into electronic publishing – be it eBooks or, indeed, electronic book readers, the more important this issue becomes.

World Rights

Usually publishers will want to retain worldwide rights. However it's very difficult to get a book that's been published outside the US, into US distribution channels at a sensible price (I've found that out the hard way.) What you need to do is try to get a US publisher for your book separately. Some UK publishers can do this through sister companies in the US. Make sure your publishers explain their position to you very carefully regarding US publication, distribution and sales and that you're happy with it. If you aren't and US sales are important to you, insist on retaining the US rights yourself. If you're not a US citizen you probably won't get a US publisher on the strength of proposals only, but you might once the book is published in the UK version. For US citizens being published by US publishers, I believe the world rights issue is simpler and easier. However you will get more information on this from Writers Guild of America or the American Society of Authors and Writers (web addresses at the end of this book.)

Book Title

Especially if you are a speaker or trainer, it's worth asking the publishers to insert a clause allowing you to use the book's title for anything else, e.g. workshops, courses, presentations, etc. I did this with

Powerwriting and Prentice Hall were quite happy to make that change, as obviously this provides symbiotic sales opportunities for the book. You might want to consider registering the title as a trademark, too. How to do this depends on which country you are in; your local Chamber of Commerce should be able to refer you on to the right resources. Also do a web search for "trademark registration" as there may well be a local website that can advise you. Finally, it's a useful idea to register a URL in the same (or similar) name as your book title. A website dedicated to your book will be very useful once it is published (see below) and the sooner you register the URL the better.

Editing

Be careful that you retain some freedom to dispute an editor's changes. I have had a couple of very bad experiences with editors (external freelancers, often used by publishers) who didn't understand and weren't interested in my content and changed things erroneously. Fortunately the publishers listened to me and disallowed the editors' changes, but largely that was because I had retained the freedom to dispute editors' manuscript changes in the contract.

Termination

It's perfectly reasonable that a publisher should retain the right to terminate the agreement if you do not deliver according to the terms of the contract. But in one draft publishing contract that was submitted to me, the termination clause basically said the publisher could terminate the contract even if I did everything right, and that they could commission another writer to do a book on the same topic.

Needless to say I got them to change that before I signed... one more reason why you must be very careful to read the small print.

Marketing

Try if you can to get the publisher to specify what they intend to do in the way of marketing your book. Unfortunately they're likely to hedge around it and refuse to put anything in the contract. That's usually (but not always) because conventional publishers do very little marketing.

Author's Discount

If you intend to buy copies of your book from the publisher and sell them yourself – say, "back of room" at presentations, performances and in workshops - you should ensure that you get a healthy discount that is separate from your author's royalty. Some publishers will now set up a separate arrangement with you which is in effect a retailer's agreement. If you intend to promote your book from your website you need to make a business decision based on whether it will be more profitable to buy in copies from the publisher and sell them direct from your site (don't forget you have to charge for and arrange packing and posting too) or whether to have an affiliate arrangement whereby buyers click through from your site to that of the publisher (probably less profit, but no extra work.) All number crunching I'm afraid.

VAT (UK)

Be careful of this one. Although at the time I'm writing this books are zero-rated, if you are VAT registered you must charge VAT on your royalties to the publisher. I have an arrangement with Prentice Hall's parent company, Pearson Education, whereby they can raise VAT invoices on my behalf. This simplifies things, but not all publishers can do it. If in doubt check with your accountant and the publishers' accounts people. If you're outside the UK similarly check with your accountant on your position regarding tax before you sign the contract.

Free Copies

This is only a small thing but the customary number of free copies you get on publication is six. One publisher I've worked with tried to get away with giving me three... but cheerfully upped it to six when I complained! Also, if you are doing your own marketing for your book it's not unreasonable to expect the publisher to let you have some free copies to give as competition prizes, or for review by appropriate journals and portals. They may be reluctant to formalise such free copies as a clause in your contract but be happy to let you have a few copies now and again unofficially, and that's better than nothing.

You'll find a sample contract in the appendix.

CHAPTER 12

Writing Your Book

Every writer has a different way of doing things so there's no point in me telling you how I approach writing, at what time of day I'm most creative, or any of that other hugely personal stuff that's probably wrong for you. You need to find your way and organise your writing in the way that works best for you. There are no right ways or wrong ways – only ways that are right or wrong for you.

When you come to write the book and are faced with what many people call that "huge, impossible project," here's a trick that I was taught when shivering with fear about my first book.

Forget thinking about your book as one project. Think of it as a series of discrete projects: one for each chapter. Get that notion fixed firmly in your mind. 15 writing projects of 4,000 words each feels a lot more comfortable than one writing project of 60,000 words. You also get a greater sense of achievement as you're working through the book, because the completion of each chapter becomes a major milestone.

And how long should your book be? Well, fashions vary and much depends on how much you have to say. Novels run anywhere from 40,000 words (slim paperback) to 250,000 words and more (heavy doorstop.) General nonfiction books run within roughly the same numbers; a cook book may be 30,000 words or less, but a major historical or biographical work can run to 150,000-200,000 words at least.

Currently 40,000 words is the optimum number for (printed) business and most other practical nonfiction books. This results in a slimmish but still substantial looking large paperback book. When I submitted proposals for Powerwriting my original estimate was 60,000-80,000 words, but when I signed the contract with Prentice Hall they cut me down to 50,000, saying that busy people don't have time to read more than that. Since that time, the word count has come down again.

When in doubt, take advice. Your publisher (if you have one) will tell you how many words they want you to write. If you're self-publishing, research current similar books in your local bookstore or on Amazon who list the number of pages with a book's ISBN and other details. Very roughly, in a large paperback there will be about 300 words per page – in a small one, about 250 words. As the Americans say, now do the math...

How Long Will It Take To Write?

This of course is another "how long is a piece of string" question, but it is possible to calculate a rough timetable. If your book is being published externally, you are likely to have the experience of writing the sample chapter. This is useful up to a point, but writing a sample chapter in isolation is likely to take longer than the chapters you write when you're in full flow. Decide how many days you will need to perform the following functions:

- assembling research
- working up full notes for each chapter
- writing up each chapter

Set Goals

Some people choose to allocate a number of hours each day to work on a book. Others, like me, prefer to allocate blocks of several days to work pretty well solidly on a book, then have blocks of days when we do something else. You'll know just by thinking it through which approach will suit you better.

I can only speak for myself here and I'm a professional writer anyway, so am capable of working frighteningly fast (not good for me to do that too often though!) However when I'm working on a book I have many other things to do at the same time, including consultancy work, my workshops, plus all the domestics such as dog walking, helping with people's horses, cooking for my teenage son and his rock band, being his golf caddy, etc.

So for me, to complete two chapters a month is comfortable. Given that there is no research to be done, I should be able to complete a chapter in 3-4 days. That's a chapter with an average length of about 4,500 words.

You can build quite a lot of flexibility into a schedule like that. If you find yourself having a quiet time with your other activities, you can spend extra hours and days on the book so you get ahead of your schedule. That way, should you have a rush on with something else later, you won't find yourself behind schedule overall.

On the basis of a 50,000 word book with 12 chapters (including introduction) you should have the first draft of your manuscript completed in 6 months. You then need to allow another month to do your own primary edit (if the book is then going to be edited by the publishers) or probably two months if you're self-publishing and/or using the services of a freelance editor.

Assembling Input

Your book may not have required any research other than collating information that already exists in your mind, in which case you probably don't need to read this section. However you may still want to refer to other sources as well as using examples of your own or other people's work, illustrations, graphics, photographs, etc.

I have touched on this issue before, earlier in the book. However it's worth revisiting. If you're using other people's stuff be sure you are legally cleared to do so. If in doubt check with your lawyer or the writers' associations I've listed at the end of this book. Plagiarism and copyright infringement, despite being commonplace these days with the internet's cheerful oblivion concerning intellectual property and all that, is still a major no-no if you want to hold your head up and be seen as a credible author.

If you do collect research material then you need to assemble it and file it under each chapter of your book. Particularly if the research material is printed on paper, assemble it in the same order as the running order of each chapter. That way you don't have to leaf through piles of material to find what you want.

If you have collated information electronically, read through it all and cut and paste the bits you want into another document, so that it runs in the order that your chapter runs. Then have it available as a document called "Chapter X, background research" which you can either open in a separate window while you're working, or print out and refer to on paper.

Mechanics of Writing

Another area we need to take a brief look at in this chapter is the mechanics of writing. By that I mean how, and to a lesser extent where, you physically record your words. In my job you learn how to write wonderful words in all sorts of unlikely places. I once wrote a very good press release by hand in a notebook while sitting on an incredibly uncomfortable plastic chair waiting for a delayed flight out of Kennedy Airport in NYC.

Many times, too, I have written and edited complex speeches on a laptop while sitting (sometimes squatting if there were no spare chairs) backstage of a conference set while electricians, carpenters and riggers hauled cables and built things all around me. That old line about necessity being the mother of invention is very true. It's surprising how you can galvanise your thinking into action despite maniacal circumstances when faced with the alternative of an irate client and/or a refusal to pay due to non-delivery of the goods.

Anyway, on with the mechanics. One of the biggest barriers to restrict the flow of your words - if you use a computer to write, and most people do – is lack of keyboarding skills. Let's face it, anyone's creative flow is going to be severely hampered if they're trying to record it with two awkward fingers, eyes frantically darting around searching for the right keys.

There are endless computer courses available to people in most cities and larger towns and some just focus on keyboarding and text management skills, rather than a longer all-inclusive menu of other forms of computing that you don't necessarily need to know. If you write quite a lot, taking such a course is probably well worth your time and effort.

One of the most useful things I did when I was in my late teens (and I didn't do too many useful things then, believe me) was to take a typing course. Of course that was in the dim, dark ages. But now, if you don't want to go somewhere else for instruction, an alternative is to learn online. Courses such as "Mavis Beacon Teaches Typing" (available at the time I'm writing this via *www.mavisbeacon.com*) are effective and convenient.

Mind you if you're using any other configuration of keyboard or one of the stylus-based systems then forget the last few lines. As I write this the current bijou computerettes (many masquerading as telephones) are no doubt incredibly convenient, but in their minute compactness they do not encourage fluency for the serious writer. For us lot, the terribly unfashionable full-sized keyboard still works more efficiently, because we can express ourselves on it comfortably with our grown-up, full-sized fingers.

And Dictation or Voice Recognition Systems?

I have yet to meet a writer – business, fiction, print, film or otherwise – who is able to dictate their works in a way that results in anything that even vaguely resembles the final draft. One supreme exception to that was the work of an amazingly prolific fiction writer in the UK called Dame Barbara Cartland, who dictated literally scores of romantic novels into a tape machine, had them transcribed and then, I assume, edited them a bit.

While Barbara Cartland's novels still sell well today they do not represent what I would call good examples of how to go about compiling material within the nonfiction world. I have never succeeded in dictating anything other than garbage into a machine and although old-fashioned business people were groomed to dictate pompous letters to secretaries in comedy films of the 1950s, I think anyone serious about writing well for nonfiction books should avoid voice-led initiation unless they are very good talkers. By all means try it, but before investing time and money into an elaborate voice recognition system, in your shoes I would, if possible, try one out over a period of time and see if it really is as much of a time saver as all that.

I tried one of these systems and although I had a lot of fun jabbering into it and watching all this nonsense appear on the screen, I found that by the time I had cleaned it all up and re-arranged it into something half sensible it would have been faster to write the piece from scratch via my fingers on the keyboard.

Dictating

In my view, unless you have the unswerving talent of someone like the late Dame Barbara Cartland (see above) dictating is probably a bad idea. The fuss and bother of dictation, transcription, printing out, editing, re-editing and regurgitating will only be beneficial to you if you can afford a very competent secretary who can do all the – very time-consuming – donkey work.

Where this technique comes into its own rather more is if you're working with a ghostwriter, who may well interview you and record your responses for later transcription. That is probably more efficient, as in any case the ghostwriter will edit your material mentally as s/he goes along without the need to transcribe every single word.

Handwriting

All I can say about handwriting is, good luck! That's probably because I have been brought up on keyboards since an early age and as a result my handwriting is worse than our family doctor's and would give any graphologist nightmares.

Handwriting may be old-fashioned now, but actually it can be a very handy tool for jotting down ideas, reminders, questions, etc. in the absence of any appropriate piece of technological wizardry. By the time you've fiddled about with your handheld mobile device, especially if you're standing in a subway/tube train or waiting for a bus in the rain, you could easily have scrawled a note to yourself on the back of an envelope.

Some people still do write their entire manuscripts out by hand – especially novelists, poets and romantics who feel they lose touch with their emotional side if there is anything more high-tech involved than a pad of paper and a fountain pen. If you are one of those, just be sure to hire an efficient personal assistant who will need to do a great deal of typing...

Backing Up

Anyone who uses a computer knows – possibly from having learned the hard way - that it's important to back up important files in case of technical failure or other gremlins. There are numerous devices available on the market that allow you to do this, whether it's backing up on to disc locally, or by emailing your files to an online backup service.

What I do is ridiculously simple, but seems to work. I email my files as attachments, to my own Hotmail account. Should the original documents on my computer become corrupted I can retrieve the last backup version from anywhere in the world, which is a comforting thought.

I do this back up process at the end of each day's writing, so if the worst come to the worst I will only have lost one day's work.

It's easy, and it's free...

Suzan St Maur

CHAPTER 13

Getting Into The Right Frame of Mind

If you're anything like me, sometimes you'll find it hard to kick-start yourself and get into writing mode. If you're writing at home this can be even harder, because there are endless distractions around the place for you to procrastinate with… housework, dog walking, gardening, cooking, eating, you name it.

Often I find that the problem is not that I don't want to start writing, but that I don't know where to start, and so find it hard to concentrate my efforts in a productive direction. If you have the same problem from time to time, here are a few ideas that may help you.

How To Concentrate

This trick helps you take the pressure off yourself, if only in your imagination. Don't think, "I've got to write the whole of this chapter now," but instead think, "if I had plenty of time, what are the key points of the chapter that I would start with?" By making yourself mentally step outside the current problem, you find yourself looking back into it as a relaxed observer rather than as the harassed participant. It sounds like psycho-babble, but it works.

Get rid of all the clutter in your mind – by crossing feng shui with meditation techniques. If that car alarm down the street is still going off, go and sit quietly somewhere other than at your desk. At the risk of offending some of you, the restroom is a good choice. Yes, even in a cubicle, sitting down. I've done some of my best thinking and got some of my most useful ideas in precisely these surroundings. (And I've heard all the jokes about that, too.) I think it's because you're cocooned in a small, plain space with absolutely no external mental stimulation. That frees your mind to focus on what you want it to focus on. If the restroom doesn't appeal to you, then sit quietly somewhere else and close your eyes. Discard irrelevant thoughts one by one as they occur, and keep nudging yourself back to the key points of the chapter you want to work on. Don't "rack" your brain; just let it work by itself. Soon you'll find things settling into place and you'll be able to prioritise and organise your thoughts.

How To Deal With Writer's Block

Writer's block is no artsy cliché – it can be a real pain that holds you up for expensive hours. The blank screen or piece of paper has terrified even famous authors for generations and we poor nonfiction authors suffer just as badly. And unlike the famous authors of old we usually haven't got time to seek inspiration through bacchanalian debauchery or an uplifting stroll amongst "a host of golden daffodils," because we have schedules to keep and deadlines to meet.

This is the next step beyond not knowing where to start with your writing – it's not being able to write a single word, not even key points. It's one of those awful times when you get mentally (and always temporarily, by the way) paralysed, and you have to be careful that you don't compound the issue by worrying *if* you might get writer's block. That way, you'll develop the "fear of fear" syndrome which is even more unproductive.

Panicking already? Don't worry, help is at hand.

First of all, another book in this fine Publishing Academy stable, "Blocks: The Enlightened Way To Clear Writer's Block and Find Your Creative Flow" by my talented colleague Tom Evans, is a seriously worthwhile purchase if you have any qualms about the issue as it goes into every aspect of writer's block not only from the psychological point of view, but also right down to rethinking your diet and exercise so you're as fit as you can be for your writing project mentally, physically and every other way.

In the meantime, however, here are a few tricks that I have learned through experience, and they work for pretty well everything you may need to write – whether it's a nonfiction book, or merely an email.

Don't Try To Get It Right First Time

One of the mistakes we all make is that we try to get it right first time. No matter how much we might experiment with a message or concept in our minds, the first time we commit that to screen or paper, by golly it's got to be perfect. This is foolish, because it steers you straight into writer's block.

There is no need to practise economy if you're using a computer to write. Screen space is available on a pretty well limitless basis and all it costs you is the power bill (and then only if you're self-employed.) Even if you use paper, you'll still need to write an awful lot before you've used up a fraction of a tree's worth. So forget perfect and get writing.

Start By Writing Around The Point

By that I mean start by writing down anything at all. If you don't yet feel confident about writing down the key points of your chapter, don't try. Instead write *about* the subject matter of that chapter. What you want it to achieve... what your readers will want to know more about... how you want your readers to feel when they have read it... and so-on.

This removes the writer's block because now you're not exposing your vulnerable soft underbelly directly to that frightening foe called "readers." For the moment you're just writing notes to yourself which normally doesn't cause a block problem. However this writing is still very productive. You're working through the content development process by writing down your random thoughts about it, and provided that you remain in the present without consciously trying to get on with the book itself, you'll soon find yourself writing about your chapter's key points anyway.

Keep That Flow Going

Once your writing is jogging along nicely it's time to start aiming for the actual key points and then final text you'll use. But once again, don't risk hitting writer's block by attempting to tackle this head-on. Take a verbal detour and go around the longer, gentler way.

Simply continue writing, but change direction as you go. It doesn't matter how long-winded it is because you're going to edit it later. Just narrow your focus on what you need to convey and write that up in as many words as you want. Think about your readers while you're writing. Imagine you're sitting next to them in a bar or on a plane. Imagine you're chatting with them casually and informally - sharing what's on your mind.

And before you know it, the writer's block will be lifted and you'll be on your way!

CHAPTER 14

Writing Style & Craft

Grammar & Things

Now that the mass media with its "newspeak" vocabulary has been part of our lives for several generations we really can't afford to be pompous about spelling and grammar any more. Even the stuffiest of academics has had to admit that stiffly formal writing is not clever, it's boring. They may look down their aquiline noses at the language of popular tabloid newspapers, FMCG advertising, and more recently the Internet, but that's the language nearly everyone speaks today. I won't bore you with my theories on why that has happened, but the bottom line is that English as a language has become simpler and less complex than it was 100 years ago.

And quite right, too. I've never understood why some people get so uppity about the fact that a language has evolved. Mind you they're often the same people who complain about the way that furniture design has evolved and French cuisine has evolved and then those damned real estate developers are daring to cut down eight trees to make room for six new houses along the street and tut, tut, life was so much better in the good old days.

Well, you and I haven't got time to mourn the relegation of Shakespearean English to the stage, even if we want to. We've got work to do here and now, and these days we write as we speak.

"Writing as people speak" is not a cop out. It's a faster and more efficient way of putting across ideas and communicating messages. And because you don't have the formality of old-fashioned "grammatically correct" syntax and clauses and long adjectives and everything else to hide behind, your writing is standing out there all by itself. So it's got to be strong enough to hold its own without the support that old-fashioned writing often gives to less-than-strong messages.

Having said that old-fashioned writing with perfect grammar and syntax and spelling etc. can be forgotten, I suppose this should be a very short section because today we can all write what we like in the way that we like. Well yes, but wait a minute. Rather like with golf or poker, with writing you really should know what the rules are before you can benefit from breaking them.

Now, I'm not going to launch into a lesson in English grammar here because that would be insulting your intelligence and education. It would also be intensely boring. What I am going to say is use your knowledge of English grammar, your common sense, and also your knowledge of what your readers will be comfortable with... or if you want to push the boat out, what your readers will not be comfortable with, but feel excitingly challenged by. (But don't forget that there's a big difference between being a bit shocking and burying a claw hammer in their skulls.)

What you really do need to avoid is not the blatant, deliberate thumbing of the nose at grammatical correctness such as that found in consumer advertising campaigns, but the piffling little mistakes you see in some pieces of writing, which are simply the result of ignorance and carelessness. These are the goofs that separate the professionals from the amateurs. It's the text that talks about "you" in the same sentence as "them" when referring to the same person. It's the long-winded sentence that has so many dangling participles you could decorate a Christmas tree with them. It's the absence of an apostrophe when we're talking about the "it's" contraction of "it is" and the inclusion of an apostrophe when we're talking about "its" referring to something belonging to "it." (And in the UK at least, it's the inclusion of an adverb between the two halves of an infinitive... many Brits still cringe when they hear the Star Trek line of "to boldly go." But in the USA no-one seems to mind. Ah, *vive la différence*.)

These small slips and goofs in grammar, punctuation and syntax really do cheapen people's writing and drop the writer's credibility right into the doo-doo. But the bold gestures... the one-word sentence, the verbless sentence, the folkloric use of slang and so-on... these are so obvious that no-one is going to think they are oversights. This makes them acceptable – even effective.

If you take a look at some top-end consumer advertising you'll see how such deliberate, bold grammatical mistakes not only work well, but also manage to make the advertising look classy and svelte. The secret of success here is the intelligent and measured misuse of grammar, and that's something professional copywriters are very good at. For nonfiction authors, however, remember that there's only a fine line between the slick and the sloppy and it takes experience and expertise to keep everything on the slick side. It's a lot safer to stay away from the borderline so if you want to play the brinkmanship game, you have been warned...

Spelling

Now that I have thoroughly trashed all attempts at making this book into a paragon of grammatical virtue, let's see if I can do the same to spelling. Well, no, actually. Spelling is something I value. I know that sounds very old-fashioned and stuffy in the light of modern day text messaging and online shortcuts and abbreviations. But like most things there good reasons behind what sometimes appears like unnecessary rule-following. In the case of good spelling, I believe the reason is to maintain uniformity, which leads to accuracy. The other reason why some people see good spelling as desirable is to demonstrate the writer's level of education and literacy, but I'm not sure if this is a particularly accurate gauge. One of the worst spellers I've ever known was a doctor who could write out prescriptions using perfect 20-letter pharmaceutical terms but couldn't write a postcard to his mother without 6 or 7 goofs in it. The other atrocious speller I know is a brilliant mathematician and is definitely not dyslexic.

Most word processing software includes some sort of spelling checker device and these are helpful, but not infallible. They will pick up typos and glaring mistakes but, being machines, are far too logical to cope with the insanity of the English language and can't deal with homophones or wrong words that are spelled right or apostrophes appearing in the wrong place. Many word processing packages also incorporate grammar/syntax nannies, rather like mine which sticks a disapproving coloured line under most of my work. I ignore them. Finally, most word processing packages give you the option to select UK or USA spellings, which leads us directly into another can of worms.

Many people ask me how text should be spelled for international English. My answer is I don't know. Possibly you should spell according to your country of origin, assuming English is your first language, or if not, then the way English is spelled in the country in which you learned to speak it. On the other hand, if you are British or learned English in Britain but now live in the United States and want your book to sell predominantly there, possibly you should use American spellings. Probably, though, if we wait for a while the internet will solve the problem because, through its aggressive internationalism, English language spellings will become standardised everywhere. And because the US has the rest of us by the short hairs on the internet there are no prizes for guessing which type of English we'll standardise to. Although the mere thought of it will make most British purists burst into tears, I must say I'm looking forward to the day when I can write out a "check" in the UK for new "tires" on my car and then go home and watch a good "program" on TV.

Technical Content

Another important issue to think about when creating the right writing style for a given readership is how much they know about the subject matter. This is very important, for two reasons. One, it's essential that whatever you write is no more complex than the *least* technically literate of your readers can handle. Two, and this is the opposite side of the same coin, don't teach grandmothers to suck eggs; never insult your audience by assuming they know *less* than they actually do. What this means is that you need to position the technical literacy level of your manuscript very carefully if you're going to avoid upsetting some readers.

However there are a few things you can do to compensate for the inevitable variance of technical literacy you'll get with pretty well any audience. A lot depends on the nature of your book, of course, but often it's possible to separate the technical details of your material from the main flow of your narrative, so catering for different levels of technical knowledge and indeed, interest. Appendices are a useful device for this purpose – sections at the back of your book where you include technical and other detailed or complex information so readers can refer to it as and when they want.

> Shorter sections of technical or similar text can be separated from the main text by putting it in boxes, as illustrated here!

Jargon & Other Junk

Leading on from the technical literacy issue is that of technical terms. Jargon, acronyms, abbreviations and other specialised dialect are the source of many arguments among authors and editors and they probably deserve to be argued about, because their use can be as helpful as it can be unhelpful. As usual, all depends on what readers will consider appropriate, not what the author or editor thinks is appropriate. And that's where the problems usually start.

People often will tell you that you can't remove jargon from business, professional or technical books without seriously "dumbing them down," but don't believe a word of it. It is possible to make almost any topic understandable to any reasonably intelligent reader without insulting that intelligence. It just takes a bit more effort and thought. And that brings me neatly to another point to be wary of: people, especially less-than-adequate people, love to hide behind jargon and other gobbledy-gook. It's part of that old line about "blinding them with science" and is closely related to the pompous-speak so loved by academics and scientists that makes reading their books harder work than a walk through a steaming jungle.

In a similar way, using jargon and technical terms makes these people feel important and in control, even when their readers don't understand what they're talking about but feel too intimidated to complain. Not only is that incredibly rude to the readers concerned, but it's also potentially dangerous if readers should totally misinterpret what the author has written.

I expect you've noticed how embarrassing it is when someone uses the wrong jargon or cliché and how irritating, yet funny, that can be? My own two personal pet-hates are people who talk about "panning the camera" when what they mean is move it in any direction (to pan means only to swivel the camera from side to side on the tripod) and journalists who talk about someone who has been "thrown from his/her horse" when they mean he/she has fallen off it (it's relatively rare that a horse will succeed in throwing a rider off its back.) There, I'm glad I got those off my chest. And the lesson here? Only use jargon and technical-speak if you really know what it means and how it sits within your subject, *and* if you're sure your readers understand it as well as you do.

And talking of clichés… this is another area we need to take a look at, although with the advent of much plainer speaking – largely due to the Internet – we seem to have kissed goodbye to the more awful ones that pervaded business communication in the 1980s and 1990s and wormed their way into almost every form of conversation and nonfiction writing. Thanks Heavens for that, too. I'm beginning to feel nauseous already, as I write down such pearls as "situations at this moment in time" and "within those parameters," not least of which because when people talked about "parameters" they usually meant "perimeters," but never mind. Those were rife back in the 1980s, and later they were joined by their electronic siblings like "leading edge technology," "state-of-the-art" etc.

More recently we have had such pearls as "passionate," "pathways," "singing from the same hymn sheet," "tick box exercise," "empowerment," "drivers," etc., plus of course those old perennial favourites like "situations" and "scenarios."

Once again, many of these clichés and those that have replaced them are useful smokescreens behind which people can hide for a while until they work out what it is they really want to say. They are the "fast food" of communication, propping up writers whose messages usually aren't strong enough to stand up by themselves. Yet it's very easy to fall back on these clichés – they're convenient "fillers" for times when we're not clear in our minds about what to write. (Yup – even I resort to the so-and-sos every now and again.)

People who do manage to avoid using them stand out as individuals with personality and confidence – and I don't know about you, but that's how I like to be perceived. Not that I always succeed…

Non-English Speaking Readers

The whole jargon/cliché issue gets even more complex in the case of readers whose mother tongue is not English or even more challenging, readers who don't speak English at all.

One of my more challenging regular jobs in recent years was the writing of video training scripts for the Europe/mid East division of one of our favourite car manufacturers. I say challenging, because all my scripts got translated into 12 languages other than English. Another challenge was the fact that it takes longer to say something in one language than it does in another; for example, German and especially Greek and Finnish are anything up to 50% longer than English. As budget existed only for one visual cut of the training programme, the script had to be structured so that long pauses in the English version (the shortest) fell between self-contained segments, but that the exact translation of those (for the longest languages) ran together as one continuous monologue. Technical intricacies of the script were usually corrected and edited by a charming, handsome British engineer who couldn't write a note to the milkman without getting the syntax wrong, which made the re-writing of his changes in the light of all 12 languages even more challenging for me. And then, of course, there was the requirement to produce scripts of a high creative standard, she said while foaming at the mouth. "Creative?" yelled the delightful, long-suffering German producer of these programmes, "you vant to be creative as vell? I sink you're nuts. In fact you have to be nuts even to try doing zis."

The moral of the story is, if you're writing material either for translation from English or for readers who speak English as a second language, it *does* have to be kept simple. You need to keep all figurative language, jargon, technical terms, clichés, metaphors, similes, other figures of speech, and quite a lot besides if not completely out of the picture then at least at arm's length. Sometimes you will be told by a publisher that despite your book being distributed across non-English language markets the people who will buy the book and read it will speak English well enough so you are free to write whatever you like. Don't believe this one. Ever.

The readers may speak and understand English at an academic level and even may have studied Shakespeare's bawdy jokes or Jane Austen's clever little ironies. However they probably won't understand most modern English figures of speech and certainly won't understand typical British / Irish / North American / Caribbean / Antipodean / other English-language humour. That's always the real killer. In our global village of the future we may become good at sharing straightforward information across the cultural and linguistic divides, but it will be many more generations before we understand each others' jokes.

Translation of Your Book

Although I can't really speak from experience as I only write in another language (French) once in a while, according to all the professional translators I've asked it seems English is an extremely useful language to use as the basis for multiple translations. Its large vocabulary (roughly double that of French in terms of the number of words in common, everyday use) allows you to be very precise in whatever you write, which minimises ambiguities for translators to trip over. English may not provide you with raw material to create the most exciting multi-lingual translations of your book in the world. But then multi-lingual communication can't be anything but pretty bland anyway, because it's based on lowest common denominators. At least with English you can ensure that the information in your book is efficient and accurate.

If you're having your book published by a conventional publisher, the issue of foreign translation rights will be flagged up in your contract. The usual way this is done is for your publisher to sell sub-rights to the foreign publisher in question, and then getting the translation done is their problem. It's slightly frustrating to know that your book is being translated into a language you can't speak and don't understand, but you really have little alternative other than to trust them.

This has happened now with two of my books and although I wanted to have some sort of communication with the person who was going to translate them, I was told politely to mind my own business. If you're self-publishing, or publishing with Bookshaker, this is something you may well have more control over. To me it only makes sense for the English-language author not only to make contact with the translator, but also to be available throughout the process should the translator have any questions or not understand something. It would appear, however, that conventional publishers, at least, don't share my view of this logic. Grrr.

Humour

For generations people have been saying that laughter is good medicine. And now the scientists have taken an interest it turns out great-grandma was right. The boffins have discovered that laughter releases helpful goodies in the body which boost your immune system. In fact the therapeutic benefits of laughter are now being harnessed by academia and the business community into laughter workshops and other formalised chuckle sessions. Get the workers laughing and you raise productivity, so it seems.

However it is extremely easy to get humour wrong. And a joke that's sent to someone who doesn't see the funny side will create more ill health through raised blood pressure than a few laughs could ever cure.

So what's the answer? How do we harness humour and make it work for us, not against us?

People often say that the internet's international nature makes it an unsuitable environment for humour for fear of it not translating across national boundaries – and inadvertently causing offence. But there are a couple of simple rules which – although not universal panaceas that always work – can help you use humour in your book without risk.

Use humour about circumstances, not people. If you think about it, the butt of many jokes and other humour is a person or group of people, so it's hardly surprising that offence is caused. The more extreme types are obvious - mother-in-law jokes, blonde jokes, women jokes, men jokes – but there are many more subtle ones too.

Then there are the nationality gags. I remember in one year hearing exactly the same joke (in three different languages) told by an American about the Polish, by a Canadian about Newfoundlanders, by a French person about Belgians, by a French-speaking Belgian about the Flemish, and by a Flemish person about the Dutch.

Obviously most humour is going to involve people in one way or another. But as long as the butt of the joke is a set of circumstances, not the people, you're far less likely to upset anyone. And there is an added advantage here.

Whoever they are and wherever they come from, people will usually identify with a set of circumstances. Take this one for example...

Some people are driving along at night and are stopped by a police car. The officer goes to the driver and warns him that one of the rear lights on his SUV isn't working. The driver jumps out and looks terribly upset. The officer reassures him that he won't get a ticket, it's just a warning, so there's no problem. "Oh yes there is a problem," says the man as he rushes towards the back of the car. "If you could see my rear lights, it means I've lost my trailer."

As the butt of the joke is the broken rear light and the loss of the trailer, not the policeman or the driver, no-one can be offended. And most people can identify with how that would feel.

The other key issue with humour is wordplays, puns, and anything else that's based on figurative speech, slang, or jargon. The short answer is they don't work internationally. However if the play or *double entendre* is in the concept rather than the words, it probably will work.

These may be funny to us, but would not be understood by anyone who is not a good English speaker because there is a play on the words:

- Déjà moo: The feeling that you've heard this bullsh*t before.
- The two most common elements in the universe are hydrogen and stupidity.

The following, however, probably would be understood because the humour is in the concept, not in the words themselves:

- You don't stop laughing because you grow old. You grow old because you stop laughing.
- The trouble with doing something right the first time is that nobody appreciates how difficult it was.

Beware Being Too Much Of An Expert

Experts are usually the last people who should finalise any book about what they're experts at, unless the target readership consists of experts too. What an expert thinks is easy for a 12-year-old to understand is often beyond the 12-year-olds' parents' comprehension. And there is another danger to clear thinking if you, or someone closely involved, knows the subject matter backwards; familiarity breeds contempt. Because you're used to dealing with the subject matter every day, it's very easy to overlook things that may seem trivial to you, but are very important to your readers.

I fell victim to that one when I gave my very first video scriptwriting workshop years ago, and I was showing someone the best way to write a piece of narration. The workshoppee said, "but why is it better to do it this way?" I only just stopped myself in time, from saying "because it's better, that's why." I knew it was better that way, but I couldn't articulate why it was better. I just did it that way by instinct. It was only after I'd gathered my thoughts for a minute or two that I could explain it properly to the workshoppee. Yet it was important to her, and to her learning process.

This is where a good editor's skills can be really helpful, by performing a reality check on your draft manuscript and putting him or herself in the readers' shoes and telling you honestly if you're writing at too high a level, or too low, for the readership you're aiming at. It's always easier for someone who is one step removed from a book project to pick up on issues like this. So no matter how irritating you find your editor's criticisms (and I know how it feels on both sides of that fence, being both an author and an editor) do listen to them, and remember that their intentions are entirely honourable!

A Checklist of Basic Writing Craft Tips

This is a list I have been using for many years for my business communication workshops and tutorials, articles, etc., and people have told me they find it useful:

- ❑ Write as people speak, but don't just write down a conversation
- ❑ Write in terms of "we" and "us" or "I" and "me," but don't use a pompous "royal we" approach
- ❑ Make every sentence relevant to the reader
- ❑ Don't just get to the point – start with it, and phrase it so it will grab the reader's attention
- ❑ Say what you mean and don't procrastinate with fuzzy language
- ❑ Be informal but be careful not to be overly familiar
- ❑ Use go words, not slow words – sharper nouns, stronger, shorter verbs
- ❑ Use active rather than passive phrasing ("go to bed now," not "it's time you went to bed")
- ❑ Although simple is usually better, don't over-simplify – it can seem childish or patronising
- ❑ Avoid long blocks of text because they're uninviting to read
- ❑ Visually break up long sections of text by peppering them with cross-headings or **emboldened key points**
- ❑ Don't go into more than one idea per sentence
- ❑ Write so that one sentence flows logically into the next

❑ One-word or verbless sentences are useful for pacing and effect, but only if you use them sparingly

❑ Where possible start new paragraphs with links like "Of course," or "However," to keep the audience hooked

❑ Use a list or bullet points to put across more than two or three items in a sequence

❑ Keep jargon to a minimum and be sure your reader will understand what you do use

❑ Avoid meaningless or valueless clichés because they make your writing seem unoriginal

❑ Avoid adjectives and superlatives that smell phoney, e.g. "best," "fastest," "exciting"

❑ Use the most visual adjectives and adverbs you can think of – they're powerful

❑ Use "Plain English" wherever possible and especially when writing for readers for whom English is a second language

❑ Check for small grammatical and punctuation goofs – they make you look amateurish

❑ Check for spelling mistakes and don't rely totally on your spellchecker

Suzan St Maur

CHAPTER 17

Producing Your Final Manuscript

This is where all that detailed planning and bullet point production really pays off. Already you have a framework in place, although by now it may have been tinkered with by you and the publisher, if you're using one.

If you're self-publishing – especially if this is your first book – it's worth asking a knowledgeable person (e.g. editor, writer, author) to have a look at your book structure before you start writing it up in full, and supply you with a second opinion on it. Because you're so close to the project by now you might miss inconsistencies or gaps in the flow of information, and an informed but hitherto uninvolved mind taking a fresh look might be very helpful.

Once again a lot of how you tackle the writing up of your chapters depends on the subject matter and your personal preferences. However here is how I do it, and as it works for me, hopefully it will work for you too.

Firstly I separate the chapter breakdown into one document for each chapter. I'm left with a smallish collection of notes. I then space those out (physically, using the word processing software on my computer) so that each note now becomes a subject heading. At this point if you prefer to work with pens or pencils you can print out the document so that each subject heading heads up one page, then staple those pages together in order. I prefer to do it all on the computer because it's quicker and more convenient, but *"chacun à son goût."*

Now, start writing more bullets and notes under each subject heading. Leave plenty of space between them so you can add sub-notes and sub-sub-notes. Add in the information you want to include from your research material (this is much easier to do on a computer) in the appropriate places.

Work through this process without hurrying, but keep going for as long as you feel the creative energy flow. Don't stop to cook dinner or walk the dog while inspiration is burning – get help from your partner / children / parents / employees / local dial-a-pizza. Once you have incorporated the bare bones of all information you feel needs to go into that chapter, stop and take a short break – the dog needs a walk by now anyway. Then go back to the chapter and edit your notes as necessary. The break is important; even if you only leave it for an hour or two. The fact of thinking about something else for a while means you look at your work from a refreshed viewpoint.

However, try not to leave long gaps between spurts of writing your book. With nonfiction it's not so critical as it is with fiction - there you need to keep plots, sub-plots and all your characters fresh in your mind, so you really need to work on it daily. But even with nonfiction, if you leave it for more than a week or so you'll find you have to spend some time refreshing your mind and getting back into the project before you can start writing well again.

Okay, enough with the notes. Now you need to take the plunge and start writing prose. Because you have mapped out the content of your chapter so carefully and thoroughly, you'll find that some of it has already started to write itself. Your job then becomes one of linking and smoothing, rather than having to think up stuff from scratch. This method doesn't remove the fear of writing altogether (if you're that way inclined) but it certainly makes it a lot easier.

Some writers will plan all the book's chapters to this degree of detail before they write any of the chapters up, but I think I would find that approach boring. I prefer to split up, annotate and write up one chapter at a time. There's a much greater sense of satisfaction, too, when you've finished your chapter of 4,000 or 5,000 words. I always print it out and put it in a ring binder. Seeing my work physically on paper makes it feel more real to me. But then I'm old and grew up with ancient artefacts called typewriters with which you saw your work on paper whether you wanted to or not.

When you finish each chapter, reward yourself with a small treat. It's a genuine accomplishment. OK, you may edit and change it around later, but for now it's a job well done. I usually create a wall chart for each book and take great pleasure in ticking off each chapter as I write them – in a column that says Draft #1…

Then, when you finish the final chapter, take at least a week off from the project. Go and do something completely different. Forget about the book and everything connected with it.

Editing

Now that you've had a good break from writing your book you will go back to it refreshed. Looking at your work again, you'll see a number of things that could be improved without really trying. You'll also find passages, paragraphs and even whole chapters that previously seemed OK but not quite there, will now look definitely not there! However because you're coming back into it with renewed energy and vigour, what may have seemed like a difficult problem to rectify initially will now be much easier to put right.

Take your time over your editing process. And most important of all, be hard on yourself. Put yourself firmly in the shoes of a potential reader and ask yourself if – in this role – you would a) understand everything and b) find it interesting. If the answer is no to either then rewrite the section concerned until it *is* a) understandable and b) interesting.

Don't Rewrite To Death

Many publishers' editors love telling authors to rewrite their books – especially fiction – several times. "The finished first draft is the easy bit. The rewriting is where the book is properly created."

Personally, I think that's bullshit, especially where nonfiction is concerned, but even with fiction. Too much rewriting can endanger the freshness and flow of the original work to the point where the book loses its momentum and its personality. In my view it's far better to get all the structure and content order issues sorted out *before* you start writing up the final manuscript, not after.

And for what it's worth, that approach can work well for fiction, too. Sorting out your storyline, your plot and subplots, your characters and their relationships, the main action, the red herrings, the sub-climaxes and main climax, etc., can all be done prior to writing the final text, so you're working to a very tightly detailed framework all the way along. I know of many successful novelists who use this technique, and I have used it for my (two) fiction efforts (so far.) The technique certainly works well for nonfiction as I've described in earlier chapters; plan first, write later. That way you don't have to start tearing your work apart in the edit and then try to stick it back together again while maintaining a lively and spontaneous feel... that's very hard to achieve.

Word Count

Be mindful of the final word count required for your book. If you're over by a small amount, prune back unnecessary adjectives and adverbs (something you should do anyway.) If you're over by a large amount you will need to think in terms of removing whole paragraphs or even whole chapters. It's far better to remove large chunks than it is to prune the existing text too hard. Too much pruning will make it stilted and difficult to follow.

If you're under the word count and you don't need to keep some in hand in case other chapters are too long, don't try to pad your work out to make it longer. This will make your book less crisp and lively. Instead – depending on the subject matter of course – insert examples, verbal illustrations, short case histories, charts, graphics or any other interesting material that supports your key messages without lengthening them.

Usually you can put material like this into a box so that it is seen to be separate from the main text. This way, readers aren't interrupted as they go through your text and can look at the box when they've finished reading the paragraph or section concerned.

The External Editor

If your book is being published externally, once you've finished your edit the manuscript will go the publisher's editor. This person will probably be a freelancer and his/her identity will not be revealed to you. That's probably because writers like me argue furiously with editors' recommendations and if we know who they are and where they live we would probably send the boys over to burn their houses down. Seriously… in truth I've only had two unfortunate experiences with editors who didn't understand what my book was about and in both cases their changes were overruled by the publishers.

Like it or not, most of these editors do know what they're talking about and the fact that they're not too familiar with your subject matter is probably a good thing. That's because this allows them to pick up on discrepancies and unclear passages much more easily and bring them to your attention. Also they will tidy up any problems with grammar, syntax, spelling, punctuation etc. that you might have missed.

Once the edit comes back to you, you'll have the opportunity to go through the issues raised by the editor and dispute their recommendations if you feel they're wrong. Then when everyone is happy with the result, your manuscript goes into production.

If you're producing the book yourself you don't, in theory, need to use an editor at all. However unless you're a professional writer by trade, if you're self-publishing it makes a lot of sense to use a pro editor to have a look at your work. An informed but unbiased extra expert on the case will help you sharpen up your text and will pick up on all the little details that you – being so close to the material – may have overlooked. It's an investment that's worth every penny, if only because it will ensure that your book's style and content is absolutely crisp and totally professional. You can find freelance editors through author services companies and writers' associations – some are listed at the end of this book.

Layout

Typeface/font: keep to same font throughout your manuscript. Your editor or publishers may change the fonts in production, but if it's all the same to begin with it makes their life easier. Choose type sizes for chapter headings, sub-headings and body text, and stick to those.

Line spacing and paragraph setup: the old-fashioned formula was wide margins and double spacing, new paragraphs indented but not separated from the main body, like this:

> In the past, proofreading was done after a manuscript had been typeset and a rough print off had been taken. Now with digital and other high-tech systems the whole book production process has been telescoped so that writing, editing and proofreading can – in theory – be done all in one fell swoop.
>
> Depending on the publishing method you choose, it's more likely that proofreading will be conducted by whoever gets to produce the final book. You can make this process easier and more effective, however, if you keep a check not only on spelling, grammar, punctuation etc., but also maintaining consistency of the following:

This harks back to the days when editors would read manuscripts from paper, and the wide spacing was to give them space to make hand written corrections. Now all corrections and changes are done on a computer so the wide spacing is no longer necessary, but some conventional publishers prefer you to use the old-fashioned setup anyway – including printing out on one side of the page only. This will be made clear to you either in your publishing contract, or verbally when you close the deal.

I prefer to use 1.5 line spacing with reasonable margins, as I find this the easiest format to read back when I am editing my own work on screen. If I print out some of my work I reformat it to single spacing, though, and print both sides of the paper. I prefer to preserve trees rather than old-fashioned publishers' egos.

Headings: as I mentioned above, choose type sizes for your headings – large for important ones like chapter titles, medium for sub-headings, etc. – and stick to them. If you use Microsoft Word you'll find an automatic device for headings under the "styles" section, and this can be helpful.

Proofreading

In the past, proofreading was done after a manuscript had been typeset and a rough print off had been taken. Now with digital and other high-tech systems the whole book production process has been telescoped so that writing, editing and proofreading can – in theory – be done all in one fell swoop.

Depending on the publishing method you choose, it's more likely that proofreading will be conducted by whoever gets to produce the final book.

Indexing

For years I screamed and ranted and threw the toys out of my pram when publishers asked me to produce an index for my books and for a long time that worked – they would get someone else to do it. However in our more economically-minded times, one publisher (for whom I have done four books) said, "oh, grow up and do it yourself," and I discovered to my delight that it isn't that difficult or tedious, after all.

With the possible exception of highly technical or academic books, indices don't have to be very detailed or extensive. All they have to do is feature the key points of each chapter and pick up on where those key points are mentioned elsewhere. And much as it pains me to admit it, as the author I know the material of my book better than anyone else, so I am probably the best person to compile its index.

Sit yourself down at your computer with your manuscript open in one window (or its Apple equivalent) and a blank document open in another window. Alternatively, you can substitute a pad of writing paper for the second window, and if you're really feeling technophobic, you can print out your manuscript and place the pad of writing paper next to it.

Go through the manuscript from the beginning, picking up on key points. Try to keep to one or two words per point if you can. Highlight each point. I've used bold type in the following example, but if you're using a pen you can just underline or circle the word. The excerpt I've used is from the beginning of this book...

However the goalposts have been moved in recent times. Although in the past the only criterion for the publication of a nonfiction book was its literary and/or informational merit, today not all books are published with a view to becoming best sellers so they don't have to be "good" by mainstream publishers' standards. Many of these books are published (usually self-published) as **marketing** tools and as the means to a PR or promotional end, rather than as little profit centres in their own right, and are sold and/or distributed to audiences other than the general public.

What all this means, then, is that depending on your reasons for wanting to write a book, its concept and content don't necessarily have to conform to traditional **mainstream publishing** values. Don't forget, though, that whatever you want your book to achieve, it has to be good – "fit for purpose," as the saying goes. If your book is bad, it will make you look bad.

As you will see from the pages that follow, the actual writing of a book does not have to be difficult or expensive. Provided that you can talk coherently, you can write a book – with help, perhaps, but you *can* do it. And the best news is that these days the help you need, should you need, is much more available – and affordable – than ever before. However before we get into *how*, let's first go into the *why*.

Nonfiction books and the market for them

It seems that every time you ask a publisher how the nonfiction/business book market is doing, they will say that it's awful. However when you check out actual book sales the picture looks different. Perhaps we should conclude that it's publishers who are having a hard time, not books. Many publishers still hang most of their sales opinions on what happens in **bookstores** too, which these days are not where most people go to buy business and other practical nonfiction books.

Business books get a particularly hard time in bookstores. In most of the bookstores I go into these titles are crammed into a few shelves on the top floor way over at the back by the entrance to the employees' toilets. Bookstore managers don't like the people who seek business books because they tend to browse a lot and buy little – hence the self-defeating policy of putting these books by the toilets. I'll never understand their merchandising policy. Even in other bricks-and-mortar retail environments like office supplies superstores – where you would think there's a good market for business books – you'll find them stashed away between the waste paper baskets and the giant cans of instant coffee.

I believe people prefer to buy business and practical nonfiction books from related retail outlets, offline catalogues, or online. This isn't the place to go into lots of statistics, but in the UK, vast quantities of nonfiction books are sold in places like supermarkets, garden centres, gift shops, newsagents/ stationers, DIY stores, office supply stores, etc., as well as the various online sources. But because publishers have huge amounts invested in the heavy overhead of distributing books to bricks-and-mortar bookshops, they hang on to that with their fingernails.

Some publishers are changing the way they do business, but I believe they still have a long way to go. **Mainstream publishers** are also being squeezed by the rise in the number of self-published nonfiction books on the market and increasingly these self-publishers are getting their books into the main distribution channels.

OK, so now you're left with four key points. Arrange these alphabetically, allowing a lot of space between big alphabetical gaps so you can insert more later. Then write down the page number where that key point is first mentioned. Your list will look something like this:

```
A
Bookstores, 2
Business books, 2
C
D
E
F
G
H
I
J
K
L
Mainstream publishers/publishing, 1, 2,
Marketing, 1
(etc)
```

Keep going like this throughout the book, adding new key points and adding page numbers to existing key points. Where a key point involves text that runs to more than one page, write it like this (e.g.):

```
Grammar, 124-126,
```

And that's it. Easy!

The hi-tech way ... As you would expect, technology has addressed this process of indexing and it is now possible to get your word processing software to do the job for you, usually via what's called a "concordance file." Be warned, though; it's not quite as simple as hitting a few keystrokes and in some cases (depending on what hardware and software you're using and how the document is formatted) it may turn out to be simpler to do it manually. Because the wonderful world of IT is evolving so quickly there's little point in me giving you precise online locations of where to find instructions... they'll probably be out of date by the time you read this! If you want to follow this route to indexing, Google "concordance files" and take your pick from a variety of current resources.

Suzan St Maur

CHAPTER 16

Summary

1. Plan your book very carefully and thoroughly. You will need to show a fairly detailed chapter breakdown and structure as part of the proposals unless you're self-publishing, but in any case you'll need this to work from. Take it from me - the more effort you put into planning and structuring, the easier it will be to write your book in the end. You will also save a lot of time in the long run, because with the plan it's very simple and quick to shift things around and try out various running orders until you hit on the right one. That process becomes a lot more complex and time consuming once you've written the first draft.

2. Having said all that about making the plan as detailed and as all-encompassing as possible, allow a certain amount of flexibility in it so you can move things around a bit as you go. Often you'll find you do make some changes to the running order once you actually get down to writing it if, say, you run into duplications you hadn't envisaged previously.

3. Do not regard "the book" as one vast project - you'll put yourself off, as it will seem like a gargantuan task. Instead break it down mentally into however many chapters you have planned, and think of it in terms of XX separate-but-linked projects. Have a short break and give yourself a small "reward" between completing one and starting the next.

4. Use your plan as a template for research before you start writing. From this document you will be able to see quite easily where you may need to research further, where you're particularly strong on content, and where you risk going into too much detail.

5. By all means use a mind-mapping type of process if that works for you, but use it only to help you create your book plan - not as the plan itself. The plan needs to be linear, because a print book is, and even an eBook is usually read that way.

6. Many people advise you to write the first draft as a stream of consciousness and not worry about spelling, grammar, syntax, logic or anything else because you can sort all that out in the edit. Personally I prefer to get the text pretty close to final draft stage as I go along, because performing a major edit on a 40,000 word document is a pain. You will need to experiment though; every writer has a different way of doing things and there are few absolute rights or wrongs.

7. If you're concerned that your writing style is a bit stilted, overly formal or just doesn't flow, try dictating the text working from the book's plan, then get someone to transcribe it and either you or an editor (see point 8 below), or both, can tidy it up afterwards. All but the most academic types of nonfiction book nowadays must be written more or less as people speak a) because communication of all kinds is becoming far less formal than it used to be and b) because people haven't got the time or interest to plod through wordy text that may be perfect grammatically, but is as much to fun to read as an accountancy text book. Even a business book should be entertaining!

8. Don't over-edit or over-agonise about your text. By all means tidy it up but don't re-work it so much and so many times that it loses all its personality and spontaneity. If you're not very good at writing and editing get a professional editor to work on it after you've completed your first draft - and (*here comes the advert because I'm very good at this*) make sure the editor knows how to tidy it up without losing your personality and "voice."

Suzan St Maur

Resources & Further Reading

Here are some resources you might find useful.

Publishers & Literary Agents

There are some useful listings with regular updates from this website. Mostly covers the UK and the USA. You have to pay a small subscription but if you're seriously seeking a publisher or agent, it's worth it. *www.firstwriter.com*

Fiction

FictionFactor is an excellent US-based website and ezine if you write, or want to write, fiction. Covers most genres and media. *www.fictionfactor.com*

Self-Publishing

ParaPublishing – a US website and newsletter devoted to self-publishing, run by the talented Dan Poynter. *www.parapub.com*

General Writing

Yet another very useful US website is Moira Allen's Writing World. *www.writing-world.com*

Help With Keywords

Google Adwords Keyword tool: *https://adwords.google.co.uk/select/KeywordToolExternal*

Help To Write & Publish Your Book

Great book that focuses on how to get a conventional publishing deal … "The Insider's Guide to Getting Your Book Published" by Rachael Stock:
www.amazon.co.uk/exec/obidos/ASIN/0954821955

I mentioned Tony Buzan's "Mind Mapping" earlier on as a means of brainstorming for good ideas. Have a look at his website here:
www.buzanworld.com/Mind_Maps.htm

Here's a useful tip – if you want to find people who give individual help and advice to assist you in getting your book done (for a fee, of course) run an internet search using the quote marks and words *"writing coach"*… I've just done that as I'm writing this and Google returned over 44,000 web-wide results. I'm sure it would be easy enough to check out the credentials of any you feel would be a good match for you.

For one-on-one coaching, workshops etc for "wannabee" and new authors based in Europe, a good choice is Summertime Publishing. I know the ladies who run this service and they're excellent.
www.summertimepublishing.com

And if you need a good freelance editor/proofreader, contact Philippa Hull.
www.proofreading-cambridge.co.uk

Finally, I work as a writing coach too, as well as editing people's books for them, so drop me a note if I can help you in any way… whether it's to find and nurture inspiration for your book, for help in developing ideas and concepts, sorting out your material into a good order, editing or any other

aspect of book writing... (sadly I have to charge money for these services but my clients so far think I give pretty good value for money!)
suze@suzanstmaur.com / www.suzanstmaur.com

Writers' Directories

UK: Writers' and Artists' Yearbook
www.amazon.co.uk/exec/obidos/ASIN/0713669365

Canada: The Canadian Writer's Market
www.amazon.ca/dp/0771085273

USA: Writer's Market
www.amazon.com/dp/1582975418

Australia: Australian Writer's Marketplace
www.awmonline.com.au

Other countries: (Search online for *books+writers*)

Writers' Guilds

These can offer helpful advice even if you are not a member.

UK: *www.writersguild.org.uk*

USA: *www.wga.org*

Canada: *www.writersguildofcanada.com*

Australia: *www.awg.com.au*

New Zealand: *www.nzwritersguild.org.nz*

Societies of Authors

Qualifications for membership vary from one country to another. Some offer free advice to non-members.

UK: *www.societyofauthors.net*

USA: *www.amsaw.org*

Australia: *www.asauthors.org*

New Zealand: *www.authors.org.nz*

Author Services

You'll find a variety of author services by entering the following into a search engine box: *"author services"+books* (don't forget to use the quote marks and plus sign as shown.) I don't have personal knowledge of any of them, so you'll need to shop around.

Online Networking Groups (business)

www.ecademy.com

www.ryze.com

www.linkedin.com

www.openbc.com

Also search for "online business networking groups" – there are many, many, more!

Speakers' Associations

Associations to promote and assist people who are, or want to be, public speakers. Useful resources and outlets for your book if you're a member and you are interested in speaking. Many UK regions, US regions and states, Canadian provinces (and I assume regions in Australia, New Zealand and other industrialised countries) have their own speaker associations, mostly affiliated to the national ones. Here are the main English-language national ones:

UK: *www.professionalspeakers.org*

USA: *www.nsaspeaker.org*

Canada: *www.canadianspeakers.org*

Australia: *www.nationalspeakers.asn.au*

New Zealand: *www.nationalspeakers.org.nz*

Also, don't forget Toastmasters; more than 10,000 clubs in around 90 countries as I write this. Go: *www.toastmasters.org*

Advice on Speaking and Associated Books

SpeakerNetNews is an excellent weekly newsletter primarily aimed at US-based professional speakers. In the newsletter you'll often find tips and advice on writing, publishing, promoting and selling your book. *www.speakernetnews.com*

Distributors of nonfiction articles

The following sites showcase your articles. Interested webmasters can take them from there and use them on their own sites in exchange for running a credit for you, your business and your book. There are a number of these but the two I find most effective are:

www.ezinesarticles.com

www.ideamarketers.com

And Finally...

If all else fails and you need a shoulder to cry on... give me a shout! *suze@suzanstmaur.com*

Publishing Academy Links

AuthorShock is a free blog that has been set up to guide new authors in the right direction and avoid being taken in by vanity presses when it comes to getting published. There's a free report, articles and interviews with successful authors.
www.authorshock.com

The Publishing Academy is a membership and learning website for authors that contains articles, videos, ecourses and teleclasses from a team of publishing industry insiders and authors. They also publish books including "Blocks" by Tom Evans, "The Wealthy Author" by Debbie Jenkins & Joe Gregory and this book – by me! *www.publishingacademy.com*

Bookshaker is a new type of non-fiction publisher and definitely worth a look if you want to be paid more from sales of your book. Like other publishers, they're picky though, so use the advice in this book to give your book its best chance.
www.bookshaker.com

Appendices

Sample "Elevator Speech"

Powerwriting

The hidden skills you need to transform your business writing

by Suzan St Maur

The real secrets of success in business writing happen before you write down a single word....

Nearly all business writing aims to bring about some kind of change in the reader - of perception or behavior or both. Good, persuasive wording helps, but on its own it's not enough. For your business writing to work, you need to use an additional set of less obvious, but equally important skills *before* your fingers touch the keyboard... so what you do write is always effective and absolutely right for the purpose. In *Powerwriting*, business communication expert Suzan St Maur reveals those hidden skills and shows you how to use them for business writing that's powerfully successful - whatever your objectives.

Sample Preliminary Proposal ("one-sheet")

Powerwriting

The hidden skills you need to transform your business writing

by Suzan St Maur

In our high-tech age, the written word in business is even more powerful than ever before. Yet millions are wasted every year on business communications that don't work. In 90% of cases, such failure has little to do with the quality of writing (or design/production.) It's due to a lack of understanding of the audience, and the message being conveyed in the wrong way - in other words, inappropriate and inadequate thought. Powerwriting is the first book of its kind to teach you the thought processes you need to work through before you even put pen to paper or fingers to keyboard. Then it shows you how to use those thought processes to harness the power of words for business and other communications that get powerful results every time.

This fresh new business book will provide invaluable help to the rapidly increasing number of business people and other individuals who write their own business communications. The arrival of the internet has consolidated what already was a growing trend away from the use of professional communicators. Most people in business or other activities are now on their own, other than for "above-the-line" advertising. Marketing and other training courses merely skim the surface of business writing, and existing books and courses focus largely on the crafting of words rather than the thinking behind them, which often leads to catastrophic results - see above.

Powerwriting, therefore, is targeted at anyone aiming to influence readers or viewers through their writing, online or offline, whether they're in a small or large business, government department, charity, political party, hobby/special interest group or any other area of activity.

Non-parochial, Powerwriting is suitable for all English-language markets and is also suitable for translation into other major languages as well as online/audio publication. Its style is informal, personal, and humorous in places. In effect, it is a "sharing" of valuable experience and true common sense between author and reader.

Its author, Canadian-born Suzan St Maur, has a long and successful track record both as an author (6 published books including 3 previous business communications titles) and as one of the UK's leading business communications writers over the last 20 years.

Anticipated length is 60,000 - 80,000 words. Delivery time 6-10 months from signing of contract. Full proposal, detailed chapter synopses and sample chapter available on request.

Sample Full Proposal

This was done according to the guidelines required by Prentice Hall Business / Pearson Education. Those amounted to section headings which I replicated in here with a little description under each one.

Powerwriting

The hidden skills you need to transform your business writing

by Suzan St Maur

Whether you work for a huge multinational corporation or a small community project...

...this is the first ever business book to reveal the real secrets of success in writing your online and offline communications.

Synopsis

As you know, now that written communications are so much easier and faster, increasingly business people are writing both screen and paper based communications themselves rather than delegating them to specialists.

However writing – even writing well - is only half the story.

The other half is knowing how to approach the exercise in the first place – how to structure your message, how to understand your audience, and how to marry the two. To get that wrong is expensive, time-consuming and professionally embarrassing. Yet millions are wasted every year on business communications that don't work, because the approach to the exercise – not the writing or design - is wrong.

Powerwriting will be the first book on business writing to give readers the tools they need to approach business writing properly: to define and develop their message and learn to understand target audiences. That way the writing craft skills that follow in the book can be learned in the light of an accurate, realistic and positive background – the key to success in all forms of non-social communication.

Competition

None. All existing books on business writing focus on the craft. Powerwriting also teaches the craft of writing, but as the end product of effective research, planning and thought, rather than the starting point. As such, Powerwriting's content could even complement that of craft-focused books.

Market/audience

Powerwriting is not aimed at professional writers (copywriters etc) and is not aimed at other people wishing purely to write consumer advertising copy – that is an even more specialised discipline and there are several books out there already dealing with that.

However contrary to popular belief, advertising forms only a relatively small part of the total business communication mix. Today, the role of advertising is purely to sell product/service through online or offline media to the customer. The remainder of business communication covers:

- All the online and offline communications a business has with its customers other than upfront advertising (service, instructions, packaging, brochures, leaflets, catalogues, ongoing CRM, upselling, etc)

- All the online and offline communications a business has with other key groups/stakeholders, i.e. shareholders, potential/existing investors, internal managers/executives/workers, suppliers, wholesalers/retailers/dealers, media, influencers, new recruits, trade associations, government bodies, etc.

In any case, Powerwriting will cover all forms of advertising not generally handled by "above-the-line" consumer advertising agencies and often dealt with in-house, or by other communications agencies and consultancies.

Large organizations do use professional business writers to help them with communications aimed at these "non-advertising" categories sometimes, especially when they have a major problem to overcome. That's why professionals like Suzan St Maur are in business.

However in the vast majority of cases they attempt to do most of it in-house. In the main they do it badly, and they know it. Hence the need for Powerwriting.

So, Powerwriting's audience is:

Business: Corporate executive, management, SME owner/managers, sole traders/consultants, professionals. Of especial, but not exclusive, interest to sales and marketing personnel, HR personnel, corporate/public affairs staff, etc. All forms of marketing and business communications agencies and production companies, with the possible exception of mainstream consumer advertising agencies (who think they know it all!) Public speakers, support staff of senior executives, etc. Companies selling by mail order/e-commerce, property developers/estate agents, businesses in the hospitality industry, etc.

Non-business: voluntary organisations, charities, political bodies, government departments.

International Market
Powerwriting is non-parochial, so is suitable for all English language markets and also is suitable for translation into other languages relevant to industrialized nations. It is also well suited to audio book and online publication.

The Internet Connection
Powerwriting, naturally, covers both online and offline communications. It is not an "internet book" along the lines of the current vogue, but a book about writing whatever the medium. Powerwriting is, therefore, targeted for the marketplace as it will be from – let's say – 2002 onwards, which experts predict will see a "settling" of the current online upheaval and which will put online writing into its rightful, important place within the overall communications mix.

Style and Approach
Very informal, some humor, anecdotes where relevant to illustrate. Some short examples and exercises. Fun to read, not a boring textbook. The author sharing her skills and experience with the reader on a friendly one-to-one basis.

Illustrations not required, cartoons optional

Endorsements
Suzan St Maur works for a number of key international business leaders, all of whom appreciate fully her abilities as a writer. Endorsements and an appropriate foreword should be forthcoming with no problems.

The 10 second and 30 second sell
See all of the above!

10 seconds:
Powerwriting is the first ever book to give you the tools you need to approach business writing properly – the *real* key to success

30 seconds:
Whether you work for a huge multinational corporation or a small community project ... this is the first ever business book to reveal the real secrets of success in writing your online and offline communications.

Powerwriting teaches you how to think before you write – and get your message to work for the audience you need to address. Then it shows you how to write that message so it gets the results you want – every time.

Delivery Information

Length 60,000-80,000 words. Full MS within 6-12 months of contract. Full chapter breakdown/synopses and sample chapter available now.

The Author
Canadian-born, UK-based Suzan St Maur has 25 years' experience as a senior consultant and writer in business communications, working on projects for both external and internal audiences.

Her corporate clients include AXA Insurance Group, General Motors Europe, Norwich Union, The RAC, Clerical Medical International and numerous others. She is also much sought after as a speechwriter for celebrities and business leaders.

Suzan has written six published books so far, including three previous business communication titles. In addition she writes for various business and equestrian publications and websites.

She is a member of British MENSA, the Professional Speakers Association, the British Horse Society, and in 1997 was elected to Associate Membership of the Institute of the Motor Industry in recognition of her contribution to automotive communications and training projects.

Background to Powerwriting

As a professional business writer, Suzan has witnessed (and been called upon to correct) countless examples of both offline and online communications which have failed through inadequate and inappropriate thinking. Now that more and more business communication is written in-house by managers and executives, the problem is getting far worse.

Yet previous books on business writing – even, Suzan sheepishly admits, her own previous titles – do not address the "think before you write" requirements of business communication with anything like enough emphasis or detail. The result is that in-house managers and executives reading such books do not realize how and why they can go so disastrously wrong. Unwittingly, therefore, existing books on business writing merely help readers to craft well-structured words on poorly-structured foundations.

Why do other books fail to address this "front end" issue – the foundations?

Presumably, all books on business writing are written by experts like Suzan. Expert business writers have lived with the ethos of "think before you write" all their working lives, to the extent that it has become a subconscious instinct. Consequently if you are a professional writer teaching non-specialists how to do it, it is an understandable oversight to assume they understand the need to structure their messages on the basis of a thorough knowledge of the audience. The trouble is, as Suzan has discovered the hard way, they don't.

The objective of Powerwriting is to put that right. It will be the first book on business writing ever to do it well, and is likely to attract a great deal of interest and comment as a result.

Suzan's Previous Books
The Jewellery Book (Magnum & St Martins Press 1981) co-written with Norbert Streep

The Home Safety Book (Jill Norman/Robert Hale 1984)

The A to Z of Video and AV Jargon (Routledge 1986)

Writing Words That Sell (Lennard/Musterlin 1989 & Mercury 1990) co-written with John Butman

Writing Your Own Scripts & Speeches (McGraw Hill 1991)

The Horse Lover's Joke Book (The Kenilworth Press September 2001)

Chapters
Introduction
Note about "bizcomm"
Stakeholders: who are they?
Audiences
When to call for help

1.Think first, write later

How to think clearly and avoid being sidetracked
Thought-process barriers
How to leap the barriers and think

2.What do you need to communicate? (Really?)

The message brief – what you want your words to achieve
The message brief
Write the brief backwards
Does this really work?
Get the realities right
Research
Types of message
One thing at a time

3.Who is your audience?

Who, where, how, when and in what mood
What you need to know
How to find out what you need to know

4.How will the audience receive your message?

Different media and how your message will be seen/heard
Choosing your media

5.Your final message

Putting the elements together into a good message structure
Powerwriting = what's in it for them
Tell them now
Forget features, talk benefits
When features are objectives
The benefit of the benefits
And the bad news is...
Assembling your message
Making your case

6.How to speak your audience's language

Approach, style and words the audience will identify with

Corporate personality and voice

The "you" angle

Simple English, please

Technical content

Jargon and other junk

Non-English speaking audiences

7.The nuts and bolts

Some tips on grammar, spelling and other basics

Spelling

Basic writing craft skills

Writing mechanics

Editing

8.Now start writing

Enough theory, let's see how it works

Getting started

The New Kitchen – at last

9.How to get the best from paper-based media

Some tips on how to write powerfully for print

Business letters

Sales letters and direct mail

Advertisements

Business documents and proposals

Brochures and leaflets

Catalogues

Instruction leaflets and manuals

Press releases

Newsletters

CVs, resumés and job applications

10.How to get the best from electronic media

Some tips on how to write powerfully for online, video and audio comms
Static text
E-mails
Text messages
E-zines and online newsletters
Online advertising
Online PR
Websites
Company online comms
Pre-recorded video
Video scripts
Video news releases
Instore and exhibition promotions
TV commercials
Infomercials
Pre-recorded audio
Instruction or training
Audio newsletters
Audio news releases
In-store promotion
Exhibition/demonstration soundtracks
Radio commercials
Live text, vision and sound

11.How to get the best from "live" communication
Some tips on how to create powerful presentations
Cut the clutter
The right order
Openers and closers
Spoken speech
Writing for someone else
Why a full script?
Anecdotes and humor
Visuals

Rehearse, rehearse

Speaker training

Outroduction

+ + + + + + + + + +

Some excerpts from Chapter 3…

"Get to know your audience as well as you know yourself"

It's easy to fall into the trap of thinking you know who your readers or viewers are. Unless you're one of them, you usually don't. And that's the Powerwriting key; to get your message across effectively and to get the results you want, you have to know your audience as well as you know yourself.

****

The point of getting to know your audience as well as you know yourself, is to know how your message will be received in real life, and what it will really mean to the recipients. If you know that, you can structure your message so that it will be as effective as possible, whether it's intended to sell, motivate, inform, entertain, instruct, or whatever. The end product of this process is always the same, no matter what – your message has to do something real for the audience, especially if you want them to do something for you in return (like buy your product, or agree to support your proposals.)

Do yourself a favour. Take a felt-tip pen and a piece of white paper, and write this down:

Powerwriting = what's in it for them

Now pin the piece of paper up on the wall of your office or workspace. That's your motto whenever you write anything that's to be read by anyone other than you, or possibly your local laundry and dry cleaners.

****

Key question 1: What does it feel like to be in their shoes? Okay, you don't need to be a Method actor and roleplay for weeks, but you need to anticipate the audience's problems, the pressures they experience, the politics they may have to deal with, their financial circumstances, and how they view the world generally. It's not enough to know that they're a pharmaceutical sales force or car drivers or bank employees or newspaper editors. That tells you nothing other than their titles. Try to find out what really makes them tick. And don't worry if you can't take a few days off to work in a staff canteen or in a newspaper office. You can achieve a great deal by simply firing up your own imagination and empathy. And yes, we're all capable of doing that if we try hard enough.

Key question 2: Why should they care about your message? Unless it spells out what's in it for them they won't care, and they'll be right not to. So don't leave that to the end, no matter how much you may feel that you need to build up to it with preamble. Preamble is powerless, especially when it's being read or heard by a busy person. If you can grab their attention with what's in it for them right from the beginning, they are far more likely to give your message the attention it deserves.

Key question 3: Are these the people who will react to your message ultimately? Sometimes your immediate audience is not in a position to make a decision singlehandedly to act on your message –

they may be the monkey rather than the organ-grinder. There will be someone else in the background – a spouse, partner, colleague, several colleagues, superiors, financial controller or other unseen third party – who may have some or even all of the say in the final decision. You should be able to determine if this is so, as part of your research or even just by common sense. And you must ensure there's something in it for all them.

****

While we're about it let's have a look at the peculiarities of the main media in use today, and how we can use that knowledge to enhance our understanding of the audience involved with each.

****

Brochures and leaflets. Brochures are not often read right away. Think back to the last time you picked up some travel or gardening or DIY brochures. Did you start reading at Page 1 and continue without stopping until you reached the end of the last page? No, and neither does your audience. Nearly everyone will browse quite swiftly through a brochure and note the key points, if they can find any. Later they will go back to sections which have caught their eye and read them in more detail. Assuming that the key points have already told them what's in it for them, of course.

****

Press releases (and the editors who receive them.) Here you're dealing with a double audience with somewhat different, but allied expectations. Before it even gets to the readers of the publication, your message will have to pass the test of appealing to an editor or other journalist. These come from a breed of humans (some would even argue that!) with a very short attention span and dare I say it, a certain sloth. Anything they receive either electronically or in print has to ring their chimes very quickly or it goes straight into the cylindrical filing tray. They haven't got the time or inclination to translate a dull and boring message into a story that will interest their audience. That's your job. And these people make bloodhounds look incompetent when it comes to sniffing out camouflaged advertising in what purports to be editorial. They will accept a plug or two for your product, service or activity, but they are actually very good at judging what's in it for their audience. If they get it wrong and there isn't enough in it for their audience, they could lose their jobs.

****

Online Communications. Although there are significant differences among the various types of online communication, there all have one critical thing in common – they're read off a screen. There are substantial benefits, too, in that while your message is on someone's screen usually it has their undivided attention. You are genuinely "one-to-one" with them and that's something you must respect – you are literally "in their face" and encroaching on very personal territory. The bad news about online communications is that your message can be "disappeared" faster from a screen than with any other medium. If there's not enough "in it for them" it's a case of one click, and it's gone forever.

There are a few more stark facts about online communications that significantly influence how your message is received. One, 79% of online readers don't read – they scan. That's a little like the way people browse through brochures. What it means is that your message must be delivered in a way that allows key points – and benefits, of course – to be picked up at the same speed as readers scroll and scan.

Secondly, when people read from a screen they do so at a rate 25% slower than they read print on a paper page. That's because, despite high-resolution screens and all the other technological wizardry, on-screen text is harder to read. For this reason your messages have to be very much more concise than they do for printed media – some experts say screen text should be just half the length of its paper equivalent. Let's now have a swift look at the circumstances in which people receive each of the main types of online communication.

E-mails. "This morning when I got into the office there were 73 e-mails waiting for me," said one of my clients recently – the CEO of a large organization. "And that's the same as most days," she continued. "My system has a feature which lets you read the first line of each one without opening it. If it doesn't grab my interest in the first line I go straight for the delete tab." People are busy and e-mails take time to open, never mind read. And normally there are lots of others there surrounding yours, all shouting for attention.

Reviewers' Feedback: Sample

This arose from Powerwriting proposals I sent to another publisher. Much as I appreciated their enthusiasm (and their offer of a contract) I turned them down.

I've included my own feedback in response to comments made by the independent reviewer too. Many publishers use this method of independent assessment and you may well be asked to go through a similar process – and your feedback to the reviewer's comments will, if properly portrayed, go a long way towards dispelling any criticism.

Does the intended approach/scope of the book seem sensible?

Reviewer: Yes. I was however put off by the title: it brought to mind an image of aggressive words with shoulder pads! I did like "... the power of words" though.

StM: *Shame ... I liked wearing big shoulder pads. They made me feel important! Seriously, I'm not precious about titles and if the feeling is that "Powerwriting" doesn't work, then so be it. However it is worth bearing in mind that we need a sharp differentiation factor in the title so prospective purchasers know it is not an ordinary business writing book. Also, I am probably going to run online and/or live training using the "Powerwriting" name, and that will afford us some symbiotic book sales opportunities. Consequently use of the same name across all would be helpful. As for "the power of words," I feel this is a useful sub-title but probably is not strong enough for the main throat-grabber.*

"Powerwriting" has a hard commercial ring to it and as we all know, that <u>does</u> help attract media attention at launch and then sell product from there onwards.

Reviewer: I'm not sure about the inclusion of "live" communications. Perhaps a different chapter title would seem more in keeping with the scope of the rest of the book?

<u>StM:</u> *I'm not sure if you disagree with the word "live," or the inclusion of the subject at all!*

If the former, in fact that is how we in the industry refer to such communications now. It's possible, of course, that the term is not used by some business people but certainly all the clients my colleagues and I work for, in the UK, Europe and the USA, use the term as universally as we do. At the SME/small organisation end of the scale the term may not be as well known, but then this group does not use live comms as much anyway. However, many individuals working for SMEs and small organisations are called upon to give speeches in the same way as those working for major corporates. If there is any doubt, I think from the chapter sub-heading its content will be clear.

If the latter, I'm afraid I must disagree with you. Live communications – particularly, but not exclusively, in business – must <u>always</u> be carefully structured and "written," even if the writing consists of notes rather than a script. More to the point, the thinking process and knowledge-of-the-audience element I stress so highly in the book are if anything even more relevant to live communications than they are to the paper or screen based varieties. A large proportion of my own work is in this field – structuring and writing live communication from speaker to audience, often in *parallel with related material like CD-ROMs and print. Live comms form a major part of most large businesses' communications programs covering conferences, launches, presentations, seminars, workshops, training sessions, "business theatre" etc. These events often represent the biggest spend of the comms budget, with the possible exception of "above-the-line" advertising.*

Are the contents logical, with subjects covered in a sensible and useful order? If not, what modifications would you recommend?

Reviewer: Yes, it flows nicely from preparation to language/grammar to business communication to social communication. It was good to see chapter 15 ("When to call in a professional").

StM: Thank you! Actually I was unsure about Chapter 15, as I wouldn't want readers to think that I am promoting the employment of me and my competitors, but as you feel this is appropriate I am only too pleased to include it. (And so is my bank manager.)

Reviewer: I hope that chapter 8, "paper-based media", will be clearly split into different types; for example, newsletters, marketing, CVs.

StM: Yes, indeed it will. However, "marketing" as you know is an umbrella term for many activities, not a communication type on its own. I could, of course, re-categorise paper-based material into purposes like corporate, marketing, recruitment/employment, etc., but that would lead to duplication. It is probably better to leave this chapter as it is now, categorised by type, as you say.

Are there any glaring omissions? Have things been included that are unnecessary?

Reviewer: Only the "live" communications part. It seems to make sense to include hints on writing material for presentations or speeches but I was irritated by the inclusion of anything to do with presentation delivery.

StM: I'm sorry you were irritated by that – you're obviously a good presenter and don't need any tips! Sadly many business people are awful at presenting and, even as a lowly writer, I am frequently asked by speakers for whom I write to advise on delivery techniques as well. Often, too, the two elements (creating the speech, then delivering it) are indivisible, so my feeling is that some guidance on delivery should be included in the book. However I intend to suggest that people take a course on public speaking if they feel they need more than the basic information that I will provide. When time or money for this are not available there are quite a few other, cheaper and faster ways for people to learn good speaking techniques, and I will be sharing information about that too.

Do you think the level is right for the intended reader (general level adult interested in improving the effectiveness of their business writing)? If not, what needs modification?

Reviewer: The level is absolutely right. I really enjoyed the conversational style and tongue-in-cheek remarks. Examples and anecdotes are appropriate and illustrate the points very well. I also felt that much of the humour spoke for itself and some exclamation marks were superfluous. I did not like "bless 'em" or "Ahem!" I prefer to make up my own mind when to laugh rather than be told.

StM: Sorry, it's an irritating habit I have. Perhaps it's because I spend too much time in online chat forums (I know, it should be "fora") where you need to write down your feelings and body language, e.g. <lol>, <roflmao>, <BG>, <S> and worse... Anyway, one thing we business writers have always been taught is to write as you speak, which I do and which I always teach others to do. Perhaps you are referring to a section I wrote about advertising agencies and their staff, and they certainly do need to be told when to laugh. However I will try to avoid "asides" and extraneous punctuation in future. (!!)

Reviewer: The writing style has tremendous energy and pace and I liked it a lot. It kept me going and made me want to continue to read.

StM: Thank you. I really do enjoy writing – and I think it shows.

From what you can see, does the author know what s/he is talking about? Would you regard him/her as qualified to write the book?

Reviewer: Yes, I was absolutely convinced that Suzan has masses of experience and has been able to give advice to others in the past.

StM: I have been doing my job for more years than I care to admit to and am quite well known in my own industry. I have written three published books on business comms already – two about writing - and I have given numerous workshops on the subject which always seem to go over well. Also I have served on various relevant committees (Writers' Guild of Great

Britain Chair of Corporate TV, IVCA Freelance, etc) so I assume I must be doing something right...

Will the book appeal to our target market – do you think there is a market for this title?

Reviewer: Yes to both. The writing is sharp enough to give immediate benefits and entertaining enough to make me want to read more.

StM: I believe that people learn more (and more effectively) if they are entertained whilst being informed. Anyway, writing should be enjoyable. The reason why many people do not enjoy writing, especially for business, is because they don't know how to approach it in the first place – hence the need for this book, which teaches them the approach as well as the craft.

What competing titles do you know of, and how does this proposal compare with these titles, from what you can see?

Reviewer: There are probably other similar books around but I haven't noticed them.

StM: There are a number of books on business writing, but none of them (not even my own two previous titles) gets to grips with the thinking process and understanding of the audience in anything like sufficient depth. As I say in my proposals, these other books assume too much and consequently teach people how to craft words well but on inadequate/inappropriate foundations, which is why they don't achieve good results – or get noticed.

Are there any other features we should be including to make our title even more competitive? If so, what are they?

Reviewer: I can't think of anything else I would like included.

StM: I don't think I have missed anything, but if you should think of further areas that must be covered, they can be incorporated easily.

The anticipated price is £8.99 (for 192 pages). Does this seem reasonable/competitive?

Reviewer: Yes, although £7.50 would be even better!

StM: I'm not qualified to comment on this, so I'm happy to be guided by you.

Is there a particular time of year when this book should be published?

Reviewer: No. Business people write throughout the year.

StM: Very much so. In the past businesses tended to have "quiet periods" over the summer months but this is no longer the case. Pretty well everyone else writes year-round, too, including people in non-business categories to whom the book will appeal (e.g. charities and other non-profit organisations, professional practices, political parties, local and regional government departments and agencies, etc.)

Overall, would you recommend that we publish this?

Reviewer: Yes – I'd probably buy it!

StM: Thank you again – for that recommendation, and for all your other kind comments.

Something A Bit Different: An Autobiography Proposal

The following book has yet to be published, and it's not surprising in many ways as its subject matter is potentially very controversial. The author concerned approached me to help her edit the book (she has written it in full) and get it out to publishers and we're still trying! I feel strongly that it's a story that must be told. Although we haven't had any offers from publishers yet, we have had some nice compliments about the proposals and they way the proposition is set out.

Just One Of God's Creatures

Description

Genre: Autobiography

Authorship: By XY with Suzan St Maur

Audience: Christian adult / General adult

Transgender / transsexual individuals

People with a professional or social interest in transgender issues

Market: All English language territories

Foreign languages: suitable for translation

Word count: 60,000 words approx.

Current state: First draft written in full

Illustrations: None required

Uniqueness

The first book to uncover the unusual and often uncomfortable relationship between the transgender issue and the Christian Faith: it also documents strong evidence to support the biological (rather than psychological) causes of the condition.

Contact

Suzan St Maur (details)

Synopsis

One doctor's diagnosis turned XX's life inside out, changed it forever, and nearly killed him several times over.

X was a Christian and attended church with his young family. That diagnosis and its consequences were to go against all that he was brought up to believe in. However, to protect those he loved, especially his two sons, he felt he had to take such dramatic action.

From the day X was born in YY 19ZZ, his life was one of distress and bouts of ill health. This resulted in hospitalisation on several occasions. He was always the sickly child that got bullied throughout most of his school years. Until X took matters into his own hands, trained in martial arts and rose to a level where he became the school's Head Boy - and turned the tide of suffering in favour of himself and his bullied peers. No one would dare bully X ever again.

At around twelve years old his sex drive became his master, and led X into uncontrollable bouts of violence. Unable to understand at such a young age what was happening to him, he took to self-harm. He slashed his arms as a way of releasing his pain and confusion, and took dangerous quantities of medication.

At all times, X was pondering the question why God had allowed this to happen.

Doctors failed to understand why he acted this way and why he showed no ill effects or organ damage from the excessive medication he took.

X married at 21 in the hopes that a normal life would calm him down and bring him stability. Within six months of marriage pressure was applied to start a family as a cure-all for X's troubles, and his wife's biological clock was ticking. X was unsure, but his wife's desire for a child was heavily supported by their GP – who had his own agenda that clearly did not involve X.

This externally happy family life was, internally, a living nightmare for all concerned. X's violence and unpredictability seemed to come from nowhere. It raged within him and out towards his family like a furious, uncontrollable beast. Why had God allowed this invisible, unidentifiable monster to enter his mind and body?

Increasingly tortured and confused, X ended up in psychiatric hospital. He soon realised that all was not what it seemed and a conspiracy was at work.

He planned and executed an escape, but was captured by the local police and promptly marched back to hospital - with frightening consequences. In order to control him, medical staff gave him drugs upon more drugs until X was no longer aware of what was happening to him.

Very soon, the reason for the monster's presence inside X was to become clear, to his doctors at least. This was the diagnosis that was to turn his life upside down and put heart-wrenching pressure on his family:

"You should have been a woman."

By now X needed some respite and was able to go and stay with his mother in London. She noticed that her son seemed to be producing hips and was taking on a distinctly feminine shape.

Despite the fact that his mother was very unwell herself, she managed to persuade XXX Hospital to review X's case as a matter of urgency. The panel of psychiatrists recommended that X should go *cold turkey* to flush all the drugs out of his already frail and toxic body.

During this period X lost his job in electronics and devoted all his time to searching for answers to his confusion. He spent hours in college libraries and bookshops hoping to discover the magic answer - why was his sex drive so damaging, mentally and physically? He pondered again why God had allowed such destruction to invade his life.

By now X had begun to take an interest in makeup and women's clothes. This only added to his confusion. It was suggested to him that the treatment he had received at the psychiatric hospital had so traumatised him, it could be partly to blame for the complete shift in his behaviour.

Finally, in 19XX, X was diagnosed as suffering from '*Classic Transsexualism*' and he was offered three options for treatment. One, was to remove part of his brain. The second, was aversion therapy using electronic shock treatment and induced vomiting. The third, was hormone therapy. X persuaded Dr. Y, his specialist, to take a more scientific approach through trial and observation while using this third treatment option. Within three weeks of starting oestrogen therapy, X's physical and mental conditions had improved significantly.

X realised that at the time there was little known information on the effect of male to female transition. His specialist was highly dismissive of X's concerns and refused to offer him any kind of instruction or understanding of his emotional condition. In fact his attitude to X was downright scornful. X got the distinct impression that the specialist's interest was largely academic, with himself being a convenient guinea pig. The emotional side of the story was to remain X's problem; the best advice the specialist could offer was to insist that X begin wearing "frocks."

Naturally X was not prepared for such a brutal handling of his case, and felt even further out in the wilderness than he was previously. His pleas for information and support fell on deaf ears. His one consoling prayer was "God, whatever happens to me, please don't ever let me go."

At his specialist's clinic, X was given a foul cocktail of hormone therapy. His kidneys and liver began to fail. Aware of how ill he had become, X went for help at the casualty department of his local hospital. They refused to treat him for a hormone overdose and turned him away. He then tried the casualty unit at the hospital where he attended for the genital reassignment clinic; they refused help also.

Every avenue took X on an ever darker and lonely journey, betrayed by those whom he was taught to look up to and respect. The only option left for X now was, somehow, to help himself.

At every corner X was laughed at and mocked for his changing appearance. In defence he took on local street gangs and ended up in numerous battles, still unable to control his violent outbursts.

Knowing that life as a woman was the only safe way forward, X made the decision to become XY. He was encouraged to take the plunge when the Tula Cossey Story 'Bond Girl Was A Boy' broke, but in turn it plummeted X into further depression. He felt he could never compete with the good looks of Tula.

As X made his transition to XY (his mother chose the feminine name,) he became aware of the destructive effect this was having on his family – particularly his sons. In their best interests, he decided the right thing was for him to leave. At last they would be spared the danger of his violent outbursts and their bizarre but life-saving cure: oestrogen therapy that was changing their Dad into a woman.

Of course, conventional employers at that time were frightened of the unknown and so were unwilling to employ a "male-female hybrid." Needing money to support herself, her medical condition and her family, XY had to make her living as and how possible. She had little choice but to work on the seamier side of life in London, until her looks and health became "acceptable" to society again.

XY lived as a woman for many years, during which time she went through a number of cosmetic operations to make her look more feminine. At last, the time came for her to have the long-awaited gender surgery. Then another bomb blew up.

The surgery went hideously wrong. And that disaster was followed by an embittered battle with her health insurance company over the issue of corrective surgery. Through sheer faith and inner strength, XY managed to bring the insurance company's unsympathetic actions to the notice of the public, when she explained the story on a popular UK daytime TV show.

Although her difficulties prevented her from progressing up the career ladder as fast as she deserved, XY was still driven by her enduring strength and faith in God. Too ill at the time to cope with fulltime employment, she enrolled as a mature student on a degree course in business studies at XXX University in YYY. There she so impressed them with her abilities, she was appointed a 'Student Governor,' meeting and working with many British dignitaries. Post-graduation she went on to a successful career in sales and marketing and soon was offered a Fellowship with the Institute of Direct Marketers.

XY's story is of one of extreme courage over adversity, both mentally and physically. It is a roller coaster ride of extreme highs and lows both for XY and those who love her. It is a story that will leave you crying and laughing simultaneously at many moments during her journey of discovery.

Recently XY's doctor has asked her to run workshops on this complex aspect of human life, to help trainee doctors understand it better. Naturally she accepted and is glad of the opportunity to spread her accurate, but hard-earned knowledge.

In 200X XY was welcomed into a local church, and in 200Y became a member. At long last, she was back in a much-missed spiritual home - in a church where she is loved, and where she has found a new mission in life: to reach those like herself, with the gospel.

In 200Z an MRI brain scan revealed a right-sided brain lesion likely to have been there since birth. New knowledge and technology have indicated that this brain lesion probably is the root cause of all XY's nightmares; a purely biological cause, and a far cry from the myths about transsexualism most people mistakenly believe.

And most importantly of all, against all odds XY has managed to restore her relationship with her sons, who are now grown men. In protecting her children she has indeed saved herself. God has brought His creatures back together.

Prologue
(written by XY, edited by me)

Imagine being a Christian and being thrown into a situation to which there are no answers ... then to find that your Christian brothers and sisters now view you as demon possessed?

It feels like being cast out onto the open sea in a rowing boat with no oars and no way of navigating back to safety.

From 19XX until August 200Y, this was my life. Yet God was true to my prayer back in 19ZZ, in which I asked Him 'never to let me go, no matter what happens to me.' He did not disappoint me, but those early years were full of darkness and much despair.

Even now, in the 21st century, my Christian brothers and sisters find it hard to show trust in me. Yet their children run to me for cuddles with no fear, only with anticipation – knowing that Auntie XY is a fun person to be around. I suppose I am still young at heart. Perhaps children recognise that 'youth leader' quality in me – a much-loved activity I carried out at our local Baptist Church when I was in my teens.

During my life's journey, many Christian folk from varying denominations have begged me to join their specific church ... then pulled back from the offer when they discovered my background.

In fact one Christian lady said that it's OK if I spent the rest my life as a single person rather than marry a man. Perhaps if we lived in Old Testament times this might be true, but thanks to God, when Jesus died on that cross the temple curtain was torn in the middle. The symbolism is that anyone can come to God through Christ our mediator and our Lord, and that includes me.

If anyone asks, there are two biblical references that, for me, say it all. We would all be wise to remember them as they are shown below – and they will always be with me, lodged in the depths of my heart. Thank you Lord!

We then followed this with chapter list with brief descriptions plus a sample chapter from XY's book, and short bios of us both.

Sample: Another "How To" Book

And finally, proposals for another business book which I believe will be published soon after this title. This is a co-authorship project with a business writer/trainer based in southern Africa.

Successful Business Writing In English

By Suzan St Maur & FG

A vast gap in the market

In recent times, as you know, huge new markets for business have opened up all over the world. Because of their obvious multi-lingual nature – allied to a need to communicate effectively – a common language in which to do business has become vital.

With 600 million people in the world already speaking English as a second language (interestingly, only 500 million speak it as a first language) ... and English recently having been declared "the accepted business language of Europe today" by Ernest-Antoine Seilliere, president of the French employers' association UNICE ... it's not surprising that English is now the no 1 global business language.

And this has uses within countries as well as between them. Nations like South Africa, India, Ghana, Nigeria, Kenya, etc. where there are numerous (mutually incomprehensible) indigenous languages, often use English as a common denominator for business communication at national level.

Obviously English is taught in schools in these countries and there are many conversational English courses people can take. But that tends to be all about learning basic

---

English, not how to communicate effectively for business. Such "business English" training that exists tends to have a narrow focus, either on spoken English or on grammar rules - not the formal/written communications that are, nonetheless, an essential part of most business activities.

How "Successful Business Writing In English" plugs that gap in the market

Currently there is precious little in the marketplace that shows people with a reasonable grasp of spoken and written English how to raise their game so they can communicate successfully in English for business.

Our book is aimed at the white collar worker who speaks and writes English as a second language probably to High/Secondary School standard. We are taking these people to the next level which they need to attain if they are going to excel in the international marketplace. We are also showing them how to use business English for basic marketing purposes – something no other E2L book of a similar type has ever managed to achieve.

Incidentally, our book will also appeal to professional E2L communicators (e.g. advertising copywriters, business/financial journalists, PR writers, etc.,) who want to improve their English marketing/business communication skills. However as we see it at this stage, they represent a secondary market.

Why Suzan and FG are qualified to write this book

Both Suzan and FG are extremely experienced business/marketing writers in their respective countries of the UK/Canada and South Africa.

FG has extremely valuable experience of writing for second-language audiences and teaching business English to adult groups in SA, where there are 11 official indigenous languages. This qualifies her to present material that really is relevant to people who are not native English speakers but who work in this international dimension where speaking and writing good business English will get them far ahead of their competitors.

Suzan specializes in encapsulating business and marketing writing techniques in easy-to-understand and implement formats, through her previous books which include:

- Writing Words That Sell (with John Butman)
- Powerwriting: the hidden skills you need to transform your business writing
- The MAMBA way to make your words sell
- The Easy Way to be brilliant at business writing
- plus her widely acclaimed free eTutorials, "Tipz from Suze."

Together, Suzan and FG are able to provide E2L English speakers in business with all the tools they need to get ahead AND stay ahead … something most other books and courses, simply cannot achieve.

English versus American English
Currently we are writing the book on the basis of "English" English. Depending on the distribution we can secure, however, (e.g. if we get into South America) we can make the necessary additions/changes to ensure that our material is

appropriate for American English too. It's worth bearing in mind that outside of North and South America, "English" English is usually the preferred version.

Length of book
Approx 50,000 words in keeping with the current printed business book trend

Anticipated delivery time
The finished manuscript could become available within 6 months of signing of contract ... possibly prior to that, depending on the financial package agreed.

Main markets
- ***Business:*** *White collar workers, SME / SoHo entrepreneurs and sole traders, executives and managers, secretaries/PAs, school leavers / university graduates*
- ***Training:*** *As course book / additional reading for in-house and public training courses in business English*
- ***Academic:*** *Secondary schools, universities, colleges, all connected with business studies and/or marketing*

Countries
- China
- Russia
- India
- Sri Lanka
- Pakistan
- Malaysia
- Thailand
- Japan
- Philippines
- Singapore

- Indonesia
- Hong Kong
- Taiwan
- All of continental Europe
- Trade-conscious Arab countries e.g. Emirates
- Israel
- Nigeria
- Ghana
- Kenya
- South Africa
- (Other more developed African countries)
- South American countries (?)

Elevator speech

As you know, English has become the international business language. So if you want to be successful in business today, you don't just need to speak and write English – you need to speak and write *good business English* ... to be heard and respected, sell yourself and your business, get ahead and make more money. "Successful Business Writing In English" is the only book that gives you all the skills and tools you need to achieve this – and much more.

Table of Contents
Part One: Using English in Business

1. What makes English different?

- What is English anyway?
- English - the global language
- So you can incorporate your own culture?
- Some funny examples

2. What makes business writing different?

- Writing for reader

- Bringing about some sort of change

3. Why learn to write better business English?

- Gets your point across
- Saves time (quicker to read and write)
- Saves money (shorter)
- Avoids misunderstandings and cultural faux pas
- Creates a favourable impression
- Is easier for L2 English speakers to understand
- Makes you more successful in job or business

Part Two: What Do You Need To Do?

4. Planning

- First get your message right before you write anything
- If you don't know what to say, you can't write it down!
- The MAMBA principle

5. Grammar & Punctuation

- Why is grammar important?
- Matching nouns to verbs
- Articles
- That vs which
- Apostrophes
- Common spelling mistakes

6. Creating a Clear Style

- What do we mean by clear style?
- Short sentences
- Active voice
- Strong verbs
- Personal pronouns
- Short words
- Plain language alternatives for waffly phrases

7. Structure, Layout and Design

- Make your headings and highlights stand out through
- spacing and font

- Use a readable font (include short lesson on fonts perhaps)
- Use white space
- Using visual images

8. Now let's start writing

- How to assemble your message
- How to approach your writing
- The way to structure your proposition
- What is bad writing? (some examples of sentences)
- What is good writing? (now give "afters" of above, clear, punchy, grammatically correct, relevant etc)

9. Editing Your Work

- Why edit?
- What you need to achieve
- Cutting out unnecessary content
- Proofreading

Part Three: Specific Writing Needs and Examples

10. Day-To-Day Business

- Emails
- Instructions
- Letters
- Memos
- Agendas
- Minutes

11. Employment and Career Changes

- Job application letter
- Resignation letter
- Refusing an applicant letter
- Letter of recommendation
- Welcome to new employees
- CVs

12. Proposals and Reports

- Place the main point upfront
- Write a short but comprehensive summary
- Make your document "scannable" by using headings and highlighted text.
- Create a good contents page
- Use glossaries
- Formal and informal examples

13. Marketing and Sales

- Advertising
- Brochures and leaflets
- Press releases
- Newsletters
- Websites
- Ezines
- Email marketing

14. Miscellaneous Documents

- Articles
- Technical information/specifications
- White Papers
- Etc.

15. Public speaking

- Presentations
- Business Speeches
- "Social" speeches

16. Extra tips

- Using styles in Word
- Don't forget contact details
- Try to write summary first
- Get your boss to sign off structure and summary before you get into detail
- Overcoming writers' block, etc

Quick Guide

Sample Excerpt

PART ONE: USING ENGLISH IN BUSINESS

2. What makes business writing different?

Business writing and personal or social writing (factual nonfiction) are similar in some ways. For example:

- They both provide information
- Often, they both tell you something you didn't know before
- They both bring you up-to-date

However there is one important thing you nearly always need to do in business writing, that you don't need to do in other forms of writing:

Business writing nearly always tries to get the reader to change something

This can be an active change, like a change in behaviour:

- Learning how to use new technology
- Buying products from your store rather than from your competitors'
- Using your proposals for a new business idea
- This can also be a passive change, like a change in how the reader thinks or feels about something:
- Getting citizens to accept a new employer in your community
- Promoting a famous person in the newspapers and on TV

It's important to remember that people don't change unless you give them a good reason for doing it. That reason has to be good for the reader. Not you, not your employer or clients – just the reader.

So if you want to persuade readers to change their views or their actions through your business writing, you have to offer some sort of implied or actual reward – a benefit.

Here is a useful phrase to remember every time you write something for business:

What's in it for the reader?
When you're writing for business it's easy to make the mistake of thinking about what you want to say. But what you want to say may not be what the reader needs to read. If you keep thinking about "what's in it for the reader," it will help you to concentrate on the right things.

Before we move on we should ask ourselves why this is so important.

Change is something people basically don't like or trust
Very few people like change. That's because change usually means doing or thinking something new and different, and that can be frightening.

So asking people to change without giving them a good reason – a benefit for them - is very unlikely to be successful. And that applies as much to big organizations and companies, as it does to individuals.

Business experts say that corporate change is good, and in most cases, of course, they're right
Without change our businesses and social lives wouldn't progress at all.

However, big organizations sometimes use the word "change" to conceal things nobody likes - for example, job losses. "Change" is used by utility suppliers and product manufacturers, as an excuse to raise prices. "Change" is used by technology manufacturers as a way to make us buy upgraded or new systems, whether we really need them or not.

So it is not surprising that many business people and even whole companies are afraid of change. It's a natural reaction.

For any business message to succeed it has to overcome that fear and dislike of change – whether on an individual level, a corporate level, or both.

Tell them now
Another thing good business writing has to do is to say "what's in it for them" as soon as possible.

Never leave that to the end or even the middle of a piece of business writing. Unless the reader knows right away why they should care about your message, they won't bother to read any more of it.

Look at these two examples of how a business letter starts:

Dear XXX,

Re: XYZ product
With reference to your XYZ product which I purchased from the Joe Bloggs Superstore approximately two weeks ago, I have been using the product extensively and I feel it necessary to bring to your attention that it is cause for some concern...

Dear XXX,

Re: XYZ Product – potentially dangerous
I'm sure you would want to know immediately that my XYZ product, purchased 2 weeks ago, is potentially harmful and could injure someone...

Now, if you were the busy Customer Services manager of the manufacturing company, **which of those two messages would get your attention faster?**

What gets the attention here is that the letter is about something that could be very serious. You mustn't insult the Customer Services manager by suggesting it's his fault, of course. Well, it isn't – he doesn't make the product! The benefit you offer him is knowledge – knowing about the problem and being able to do something about it *before* it becomes serious.

(etc...)

Sample Publishing Contract

This is a real contract (not for Powerwriting) with names removed to protect the innocent! It was in accordance with English Law. However I believe publishing contracts in most countries are very similar. To find out for sure, contact the Writer's Guild or Authors Society in your country and ask their advice.

AGREEMENT Dated XXth of XZXXXX 200X

1.   Parties

(1) **XXX Publishing Ltd.**, 1 XXX Court, XXX Road, ("the Publisher").

(2) The person named in Schedule 1 ("the Author")

2.   Definitions

The following terms shall have the following meanings:

2.1   " Rights": The exclusive right to publish, distribute, sell, reproduce, communicate to the public and exploit the Work in printed book format for the complete or any part or parts of the Work, in all languages throughout the Territory for the Term together with the right to authorise third parties to do all or any of the same.

2.2   " Specification": the detailed specification for the Work agreed by the Author and by the Editor and set out in Schedule 3.

2.3   " Term": the full period of copyright in the Work under the laws in force from time to time throughout the Territory.

2.4   "Territory": the Universe

2.5   " Work": the Work, the provisional title, objective and Specification of which are set out in Schedule 3 and consisting of a document or series of documents, illustrations, program code and products in any media that are substantially derived from the Work. It is agreed that the Work shall be the Author's next work.

3.   **Assignment of Rights**

In consideration of the payment by the Publisher to the Author of the sums referred to in clause 8, the Author assigns the Rights to the Publisher with full title guarantee.

4.   **Delivery of the Work**

4.1   **Schedule**

The Author undertakes that the Work shall conform to the Specification and the Author shall complete and deliver the text of the Work to the Publisher in the form and by the delivery dates specified in writing between the Author and the Publisher.

4.2   **Copyright permissions**

The Author shall at the Author's expense obtain from the copyright owner or owners and deliver to the Publisher written permission to include within the Work any material, the copyright of which is not the Author's own. The Publisher will assist the Author in obtaining the copyright permission in any reasonable manner.

5.   **Editing and Acceptance for Publication**

5.1   **Editing and corrections of proofs**

5.1.1   On delivery of each section of the Work the Editor, who shall indicate any necessary corrections, shall edit it. This will be returned to the Author who undertakes to read, check and correct the Work. This process will continue as many times as necessary. The Publisher reserves the right having first notified the Author to alter or remove any part of the Work as may be considered objectionable or actionable at law and generally reserves the right to alter, amend, add to or delete any material from the Work in any manner and to any extent that the Publisher considers in good faith to be for the improvement of the Work, having prior to effecting these amendments agreed to these with the Author.

5.2   Acceptance of the Work

The Publisher shall accept the Work when the material delivered by the Author conforms to the Specification and to the other requirements in this Agreement. Acceptance of the Work contents does not guarantee inclusion in a publication.

6.   Control of Publication and Termination

6.1   The Publisher shall have the entire control of the manner and terms of publication, distribution and sale of the Work in all languages throughout the Territory. The publisher shall distribute the book through any current and future channel of distribution.

6.2   The Publisher reserves the right to terminate this Agreement at any time, for non compliance by the Author to the terms of this agreement, by giving notice of termination referring specifically to this clause, and if it does so in reliance on this clause, then the Publisher shall relinquish all rights to the completed or part completed work as detailed in this Agreement, and the Publisher shall have no further liability to the Author whatsoever in respect of the non-publication of the Work, and may arrange for another author to write a work on the same subject.

6.3 The Author will have the right to terminate this agreement if:

6.3.1 The Publisher fails to provide a statement of account or make any payment, as clause 8 requires, within 30 days after the statement or payment is due and then fails to correct the failure within 30 days of receipt of written notice from the Author sent to the Publisher by registered or certified mail.

6.3.2 To the extent permitted by bankruptcy law, the Author may terminate this agreement in the event of the Publisher's insolvency, bankruptcy, or assignment of assets for the benefit of creditors. If the Author terminates the agreement under this paragraph, the Publisher will revert all rights in the Work as assigned under this agreement.

7. **The Author's Warranties and Indemnity**

The Author warrants to the Publisher that:

7.1 The Author is the sole owner of the Rights and has full power to enter into this Agreement.

7.2 The Work contains nothing which is obscene, blasphemous or libellous or which would, if published, constitute a breach of contract or be otherwise unlawful or which will infringe the copyright or any other rights of any third party.

7.3 All statements in the Work purporting to be facts are true and any recipe, formula or instruction contained in it will not cause any injury to the person, personal rights or property of the user of the Work.

7.4 The Author will keep the Publisher fully indemnified against all losses, damages and costs (including any sums paid to settle any claim) suffered by the Publisher arising out of any breach of any of the above warranties or out of any wrongful act on the part of the Author.

8. Payments

8.1 All payments by the Publisher to the Author shall be paid as directly expressed in the contract. All issues regarding personal taxation or other forms of deduction that may be applied to such payments are the responsibility of the Author.

8.2 Royalties

Subject to the terms and conditions set out in this Agreement the Publisher shall pay to the Author or its assigns royalties in respect of profits attributable to sales of the Work during the Term as set out in Schedule 2 Part 1 and shall deliver accounts in accordance with Schedule 2 Part 2.

9. Dealings by the Author

The Author agrees with the Publisher during the Term not without the Publisher's prior written consent to prepare or authorise the preparation of any work of a nature that is based on the Work or may reasonably be considered to be likely to affect prejudicially the sales of the Work.

10. General

10.1 Whole Agreement

This Agreement contains the whole agreement between the parties and supersedes any prior written or oral agreement between them in relation to its subject matter.

10.2 Proper law and jurisdiction

English law shall govern this Agreement and the parties agree to submit to the exclusive jurisdiction of the English courts.

10.3 Waiver

The failure by either party to enforce at any time or for any period any one or more of the terms or conditions of this Agreement shall not be a waiver of them or of the right subsequently to enforce all terms and conditions of this Agreement.

10.4 Assignment

The Publisher may freely assign the benefit of this Agreement.

10.5 Headings

The headings contained in this Agreement are for reference purposes only and shall not affect the meaning of this Agreement

10.6 Notices

10.6.1 Any notice, consent or the like (in this clause referred to generally to as "notice") required or permitted to be given under this Agreement shall not be binding unless in writing and may be given personally or sent to the party to be notified by pre-paid first class post (or by prepaid air mail if one of the parties is located in a different country to the other party) or by electronic mail or facsimile transmission at its address as set out above or as otherwise notified in accordance with this clause.

10.6.2 Notice given personally shall be deemed given at the time of its delivery

10.6.3 Notice sent by first class post in accordance with this sub-clause shall be deemed given at the commencement of business of the recipient on the second business day next following its posting, and notice sent by air mail shall be deemed given at the commencement of business of the recipient on the seventh business day next following its posting

10.6.4 Notice sent by electronic mail or facsimile transmission in accordance with this sub-clause shall be deemed given at the time of its actual transmission, provided that the sender does not receive any indication that the electronic mail message or facsimile transmission has not been successfully transmitted to the intended recipient.

10.7 Name and Likeness

Suzan St Maur

The Author irrevocably and unconditionally grants to the Publisher and its licensees, assignees and successors in title the perpetual right in its discretion to use the Author's name, likeness, biography and the product of all of the Author's services under this Agreement, in connection with the advertising, publicising and exploitation of the Work, but the author acknowledges that the Publisher is under no obligation whatsoever to use the Author's name, likeness and/or biography except as otherwise specifically provided in this Agreement.

SCHEDULE 1

The Author

"The Author" means the following person or persons:

Name	Address
Suzan St Maur	(details here)

SCHEDULE 2

Royalties and Accounts

Part 1: Royalties

1. Subject to clause 8.2, the Publisher shall pay to the Author on all the receipts from the sales of copies of and/or rights in the Work during the Term by the Publisher or by the Publisher's licensees the following Royalties based on the net profits of the Publisher:

   On copies sold through any other distribution channel:

   15% of the Publisher's net profits (exclusive of Value Added Tax) for sales up to 1000 units;

   20% of the Publisher's net profits (exclusive of Value Added Tax) for sales between 1001 and 2000 units;

30% of the Publisher's net profits (exclusive of Value Added Tax) for sales above 2000 units.

For the purposes of calculation of royalties, net profits are understood to be gross revenues from the sale of the book less printing costs and transaction costs where applicable.

2. The author acknowledges that The Publisher will prior to paying these royalties (as set out in 1) above) cover the costs of production that it may have incurred in bringing the Work to market. Costs of production here are to signify any editorial, layout, cover design and set up costs.

Part 2: Accounts

1. The Publisher shall make up accounts for the Work monthly, starting 3 months following publication and such accounts shall be delivered to the Author and settled, **provided** that no payment need be made in respect of any period in which the sum due is less than £25 in which case the amount shall be carried forward to the next accounting date.

2. All sums due to the Author under this Agreement shall be paid in Pounds Sterling or U.S. Dollars as agreed between the Author and the Publisher. The exchange rate used for conversion on Royalties will be based those published by Barclays Bank PLC (UK).

3. Any overpayment made by the Publisher to the Author in respect of the Work may be deducted from any sums subsequently due to the Author from the Publisher under this Agreement or under any other Agreement between the Author and the Publisher

SCHEDULE 3

The Work

Part 1: Title of the Work

(As defined)

Part 2: Objective of the Work

(As defined)

Part 3: The Specification

(outline of contents)

This specification is subject to further discussion between the Publisher and the Author. It may change and develop and both parties must agree any such changes in writing.

SCHEDULE 4

Free Copies of the Work

The Publisher shall supply to the Author free of charge 6 Copies of the first edition of the Work published by the Publisher. Further copies can be obtained from the Publisher at cost of production plus 30%.

Your 30 Day Free Trial of The Publishing Academy

The Publishing Academy was created to provide authors with help, support and winning techniques at every stage of the publishing process – from ideas to making a fulltime income as an author.

So, for details of a very special offer where you'll also get a free 30-day-pass to the exclusive Publishing Academy members-only area, worth £15.00, go to:

www.publishingacademy.com/free-reader-trial

We look forward to seeing you there and sharing more with you in the future. So keep on visiting and learning from Suze and the other experts when you become part of The Publishing Academy.

The
Wealthy
Author

The Fast Profit Method For Writing, Publishing & Selling Your Non-Fiction Book

JOE GREGORY
DEBBIE JENKINS

www.publishingacademy.com

THE
Amazon
Bestseller
PLAN

HOW TO MAKE YOUR BOOK AN AMAZON BESTSELLER IN 24 HOURS OR LESS

DEBBIE JENKINS
JOE GREGORY

www.publishingacademy.com

BLOCKS

"Full of extremely useful and practical advice which will be of great benefit to any writer, both novice and professional."
Steve Taylor, Author of 'Making Time'

Writer's Unblocker
use liberally

The Enlightened Way To Clear Writer's Block and Find Your Creative Flow

TOM EVANS
THE BOOKWRIGHT

www.publishingacademy.com

Author, editor, humorist

www.SuzanStMaur.com

suze@suzanstmaur.com

2041212R00112

Printed in Great Britain
by Amazon.co.uk, Ltd.,
Marston Gate.